angie,
In the c...
may all your
dreams come
true!
Mindy
Oldham

The Chase

Mindy Oldham

Mindy Oldham

8233 Yankeetown Road; Newburgh, IN 47630

Phone: (812) 598-6741 Email: rosepetal30@msn.com

ISBN: 979-8-218-97854-9

Printed in the United States of America
Signature Book Printing, www.sbpbooks.com
First Printing 2024

This book is dedicated to my best friend, forever partner,
and number one, my husband, Tim.

Thank you for taking me on this journey with you.

You are my rock.

Your God-given talent is truly amazing.

What a wonderful 35 years it has been. So many wonderful memories and the promise of
so many more to come.

I love you, always and forever.

Contents

Introduction

After a chance meeting that changed the course of the lives of two people forever, the events that followed became the most amazing journey.

When Tim and I married and started our family, we did not know the course that our lives would take. At that point, Tim had never been on a turkey hunt. Once he went on that first hunt, everything changed. That hunt lit a fire under him and began a lifelong passion.

Since that time, our lives have revolved around the wild turkey.

In 2003, Tim used his artistic ability and combined it with his newly found hobby of turkey call making by creating beautiful art on the calls that he made. He also began carving. He has continued to hone in on his skills and create some truly beautiful works of art.

This book is my endeavor to share our story. Through our journey, a revelation occurred. A revelation of which we did not see coming. Along with this, there have been many trials.

Hopefully, our story will help you get to know us a little better, make you laugh, bring some memories of your own into your thoughts and, most importantly, be an inspiration for which you can relate to your own journey.

We want you to know that anything is possible. All you must do is have the will to do whatever it is you wish to accomplish.

We have wonderful memories to share. I hope to preserve these memories for our family and future generations.

Proverbs 23:7 (NASB)

[7] For as he thinks within himself, so he is.

He says to you, "Eat and drink!"

But his heart is not with you.

THE CHASE

As a pursuit shall go, the chase ensues.

A victor will rise, either man or bird lose.

A lesson will be taught in the gameplay.

To be earned and brought out a future day.

The passion is felt in the memoir told.

A story so close to my heart I hold.

As my years rise, one more bird I must score.

So grateful for the chance to chase once more.

By Mindy Oldham

Chapter 1
Life is a Journey

As I climbed the daunting ridge, thorns relentlessly punctured my skin. My camouflage clothing did not protect me from the torture of the ruthless brambles. The briar patch that I had made my way into continued to show no mercy on me. Occasionally, I glanced up to see Tim ahead of me. Obviously, he was not concerned about my location. He had his full attention on the gobbling wild turkey we heard at the top of this steep ridge.

I struggled to keep my composure. Approaching the end of my mental and physical capabilities, I was ready to give up.

While gazing to catch another glimpse of Tim, a briar branch smacked up against my cheek. As I swatted at it, I could feel it rip the flesh from my face. As sweat poured from under my hat and reached my cuts, my face stung as if a swarm of bees had attacked me. I struggled to breathe normally. It felt like someone had taken the bones from my legs.

Why was I putting myself through this torture? This was not worth the opportunity to get a shot at a wild turkey. I did not care if I never saw another wild turkey again!

Tim's voice suddenly interrupted my agony. He looked down at me, annoyed and said, "Are you okay?" I could not believe he had the nerve to ask me that question. Obviously, I was not okay. I was bleeding. I could not breathe and I could barely stand upright.

I searched for the strength to respond to him, and all I could muster up was an agitated, "Are you okay?"

The only thing I can tell you further about this story is this is the person I used to be. My journey has changed my entire outlook on life. As you read, you will see just how that transformation developed. I was not aware that we were about to embark on an amazing journey. It would be a life-changing adventure. Just as the ridge and the briar patch presented me with a challenge, so would life.

We all have a story. Our story is a collection of moments in our life. In these moments, we create memories. The above story is one of mine. I will go further into that story later. I think you will enjoy it.

The effects of the events on us create the person we become and determine the path we take. Life can certainly throw us punches and push us around. It can also be beautiful and loving. We never know what it will be in the very next moment.

Just as the trees have branches, our lives branch out in many directions and lead us to pivotal moments in our journey. These moments can change our lives forever. They all have a purpose and are part of God's grand plan. I am a firm believer that all things happen for a reason.

The people we encounter on our journey contribute to this grand plan. Some people become a stable force, a part of the foundation, in our lives. Others leave soon after they arrive. Their purpose does not require as much time with us. Each is a blessing from God. Many times, these blessings arrive unnoticed. They are to be revealed later in God's own time.

In moments when we reflect, we see those blessings and understand them fully. We observe ideal paths intersected and events which altered our journey. Our lives are part of a marvelous story. When you look at it in its entirety, you can see the true meaning. It is then that we gain an even better understanding that we can plan our steps, but God has the final decision. He will lead us as we are supposed to be led.

As we travel through our journey, we change. Our experiences change us and we learn many lessons. We gain insight into life and many times gain valuable skills that allow us to make decisions that will further guide us along our journey. Sometimes, as we travel along, the past affects our decisions for the future. All of this creates the landscape that our individual picture paints. This picture is a portrait of our entire story. Each of our portraits have their own intricate details. When we view each detail, they all fit together in their perfect place, as in a gigantic puzzle with its pieces nestled together.

In October 1993, I married the love of my life and my best friend, Tim. On that day, two individuals merged their journeys into one. I am grateful for the course of events which brought us to this point. If these events would not have occurred, I would not be here telling you the story of our amazing journey. It is a blessing that uncovers itself a little more each day.

So, who am I to share this story with you?

I am foremost, a child of God. I am a daughter to two amazing parents, a sister to my younger brother and sister, a wife to my amazing and talented husband, a mother to my two amazing daughters, an aunt of many nieces and nephews and, most recently, a Nonni to three precious grandsons. It is amazing how one sentence can capture our entire lives. For me, my family is my life.

It is an honor and, I feel, a necessity to tell our story. I would love to share it with you. It is a story of ups, downs, successes, and failures, but most importantly, it is a story of everlasting faith. No matter what happens, we hold on to our life with a relentless faith that is kept close to our hearts. My feelings of faith have strengthened a great deal during our journey. This evolution has shown me mindset plays a critical role. I have learned that the will to accomplish a goal is unsurpassable to everything else. It is the most important factor in our success.

Another important factor I have learned is the importance of giving it your all in life.

In his essay, Compensation, Ralph Waldo Emerson wrote, *"Each person receives compensation in a similar manner for what they have contributed."*

Every action has a reaction.

We reap what we sow.

We get out of life what we put into it.

I hope to document our journey for future generations to read as a story of hope and overcoming the obstacles that so often get into our path as we journey through life. I hope you will find inspiration and encouragement. A hope when things become dark and unfathomable, that you find it in yourself to envision the light and know that you will make it through and prosper. All you need is faith to guide you through your journey. A faith that only you can find in yourself.

Psalm 37:23-24 (NASB)
[23] The steps of a man are established by the Lord,
And He delights in his way.
[24] When he falls, he will not be hurled headlong,
Because the Lord is the One who holds his hand.

Chapter 2
The Beginning

To begin our story, I would like to tell you a little about each of us, about who we are and where we came from. I want to share with you how it all began.

When we talk about a journey, we begin with where it all started. Life begins with the formation of a foundation. With beginnings in close companionship with nature, our story began deep in the cool darkness of the woods. It arose from the depths of the sounds and feelings, right before dawn, the moment the woods come alive. Starting with a special connection with nature, it later developed around one of nature's great inhabitants, the elusive wild turkey.

Establishing a foundation in life begins in early childhood. Our upbringing influences the visions we have throughout our life. This is a part of the evolution of who we become as a person and how we function. Each of us has a distinct path we take. Even if there are two people growing up in the same family, each path varies. We each view our vision through different eyes, felt through a dissimilar heart, and perceived through a unique mind. The differences, when compared, can be subtle or can be drastic. It is when the paths of two people become one where things become magical.

I grew up in a very structured environment with two loving parents. At a young age, my parents created my direction. They nurtured and guided me. I was the oldest child in my family. I have a younger brother and a younger sister.

Since childhood, I have always had a connection with nature. I remember as a young girl running outside on the warm days of summer. It was exciting to feel the warm sun on my face. I would run to the barn to tend to the chickens and rabbits. My parents had created a small farm on our property. Throughout the years, countless animals have held a special place in my heart. I remember many adventures going into the woods with my brother to explore its every inch. We took great expeditions down to the creek to catch a crawdad or two. I have memories of the great concoctions we would create with quail eggs and the carefully crafted mud pies made with the perfect ratio of dirt and water.

My youthful eyes saw limitless adventures. To this day, I can still feel the excitement of grabbing onto a large vine hanging from a massive tree. My grip had to be tight as I ran and lifted my feet to see where it would take me. As I held on for dear life, I would feel the wind flowing through my hair, as if I was flying through the trees.

Those memories are the foundation of my connection with nature. They are what have always led me to seek more adventures. Those memories have made me yearn to nurture that connection. I could never have foreseen how crucial that would be in my later years or how it would shape my entire life. It would become my life and an integral part of our story. The great journey to which I would later embark required me to have that firm foundation. Without it, our story wouldn't be what it is. It would take me to places I could never have imagined.

In life, I have always been a follower. This is where I am most comfortable. I accept the way life flows around me. I am happier not creating turbulence in the waters. Like the soft waves in the ocean, I am in my element, flowing with the rest of the water, only hoping to flow around anything that creates an obstacle in my path.

In the past, my mind's perception of failure had created an environment for me where I was not willing to take risks. I always approached things in a conservative manner.

I went to college right out of high school and got my Associate in Applied Sciences, Medical Secretarial degree at a local community college. I enjoyed the courses I took. Transcription was a course that took me longer to master, but I worked hard at it and overcame any issues I had. For 35 years, I have proudly held a position as a cardiology transcriptionist. I work for an elite group of providers in a wonderful organization. Throughout my 35 years, I've had an ever-changing journey. I love my job and am proud to be a part of this organization.

By nature, I have always been a "by the books" kind of girl. Tim and my family can attest to that fact. Planning and projecting have consumed my life for a long time. Living in what felt like a box, I planned everything, including when I would put gas in my vehicle. I even planned dinners out for the next week. Once, I used to plan every element of my life, going over everything multiple times. I required all to be moving in a self-approved direction. This would create many unnecessary struggles throughout my life. I discovered that even the smallest surprise or deviation from my plan would cause chaos. This was a characteristic I was not proud of. There were some advantages, but many more disadvantages. I found it to be detrimental to my wellbeing. If I had to adjust my plan, it would cause a great deal of anguish. Little did I know what lay ahead as I struggled with these issues.

Life is, most of the time, not cohesive to this lifestyle. Throughout the years, I have dedicated myself to working on this quirky trait. The challenges that would present themselves in my life would push this trait beyond my imagination. The struggles would transform me in ways I never thought imaginable.

While Tim also grew up with two loving parents, the path he traveled was a different one than mine. At a very young age, the path he created on his own paved his direction. He is the oldest child in his family. He has a younger brother and a younger sister. Tim is very much a leader and one whom others find very easy to follow. He has always more aggressively created his own path. He has been this way since I met him. Combining his desire and his creativity, he can conquer any adversities which get in his way. His instinct is strong and one that he rarely questions. For this instinct to be so strong, I am sure he has had it from a very young age.

In that same ocean with the soft, white waves flowing, Tim is the creature of the sea, bounding through the waves, unaltered by their force.

With his self taught art skills, he has always been a very artistic person. With these skills, he has created his own path to follow. I have the great pleasure of traveling alongside with him on this wonderful journey.

He wrestled and played football in high school. For his wrestling team, he sketched T-shirt patterns. In art class, he would work on different projects, such as banners, for the school.

As I have watched his skills grow, I am in constant amazement. An artist's mind is truly unique. Their burning passion can create amazing art. Their minds flow to the beat of a different drum. They have a unique perception of colors and shapes. In every aspect, their views on the world are different.

When Tim is working on a project, his fervency for that project is at a level beyond my ability to perceive. The sheer fundamentals of 3-D art and carving are completely foreign to my mind. I cannot even imagine how to take a block of wood and create a beautiful piece of art from it.

I believe the degree of artistic ability of a person gives them a whole new way to pursue their journey. A way for them to have more control over their direction and outcomes. This was certainly the case with Tim. Along with being able to create amazing works of art for all to see, he can create these works in his mind. He sees each project in a way most people cannot. He sees them before even being physically created. These traits alone are very instrumental in his work as an artist. They are also a powerful tool for life. The ability to create something in your mind and be able to alter it in thought is an amazing attribute.

As children, Tim and I were both connected to nature and with the earth. We both lived lives that included outdoor activities, the things children did in the time we grew up. Playing in the creek, running through the woods, hunting and fishing with family and sometimes even on our own adventures.

When we met in 1990, things were no different. We had a connection with each other almost immediately. With me being 19 and in college and him being 15 and in high school, our paths should not have even remotely had much in common, especially not enough for us to connect the way we did. We were both on different journeys.

While I was on a different path, a path I thought I was in control of, I quickly found that to not be true. Up to that point, I was a follower. This experience was no different. A very determined teenager created a path, one that I never had planned on taking. In reflecting, I am sure glad I embarked on that journey with him. We had a connection which we never would have guessed would have lasted as long as it has. We were young, and we learned we shared many things in common. While immersing ourselves in nature, we took pleasure in fishing, embarking on hikes, and maximizing our time outdoors, appreciating the gifts our earth provides for us. We had many adventures and spent hours on end together, learning all we could about each other. We were each in different stages of our lives in such a way one would say it would never work. As time went on, we only grew closer together. We were on a mission to prove everyone wrong.

After dating for four years, we were ready to get married. Before we married in 1993, we searched for a place to live. We changed our initial plans, and this was the first of many plans that changed for us on this journey. As we planned, we found out that God had other plans for us. My mom had found a place out in the country that she and my dad said we had to see. When we took a trip to look at it, we knew it was where we wanted to be. Though our eyes told us differently, our minds knew it was absolutely a beautiful gem in disguise. We purchased it quickly, and the work began. We made it our home.

After being married, we were ready to expand our family, and we became parents. We were excited to add to our little family. We were thrilled when we found out we were having a girl.

Our first spunky little girl, Courtney Ann Oldham, arrived on 08/26/1994. She was the first grand baby on both my side of the family and Tim's. We got her outside and showed her the beauty of nature at a very young age. She was a tomboy at heart and her roots ran deep with nature. She was an absolute joy, and we loved being her mom and dad. Courtney was a sweet little girl who grew to enjoy the great outdoors. She was a very determined little girl, and she kept us on our toes as we learned the game of parenting. We showed her the wonders of nature and spent lots of time outside. We hoped for her to be grounded in nature, just as we were.

Four years later, we were ready to expand our family once again. We were more sure of ourselves this go-around and felt more confident in our parenting skills.

On 09/25/1998 we welcomed our second daughter, Caitlynn Marie Oldham. She was our free-spirited, sweet little girl whom we also raised up in the outdoors. She, too, was a very determined little girl. We encouraged her to grow up outdoors, teaching her about the happiness that was found there. We had the perfect property to allow them to enjoy nature, uninhibited. Their hearts were definitely right with ours. We knew we wanted them to both have deep roots with nature, just as we did. We wanted to be sure we could show them just how beautiful Mother Nature's creations were.

When they were small, the girls would tag along with Tim to hunt small game. They enjoyed working with me in the flower and vegetable gardens.

Much like my childhood, we had cats, dogs, rabbits, chickens, pigs and once we had purchased a goat. We will leave the story about our goat for another time.

The girls enjoyed learning about everything nature offered. We would take hikes and let them explore to their hearts' content.

As they became older, they would journey down to the creek bottom on our property, known as "Rock Bottom". This allowed them to connect with nature on their own.

The importance of this connection was one of great significance to Tim and me. We held it in the highest regard and did everything we could to be sure the girls understood and nurtured their own connection as they grew up. With nature being a sanctuary for us, a place where we feel more alive and connected, it was important for them to know that peace. Through our interactions with the natural world, we knew they would discover who they truly were and they would find solace in the chaos of life.

Proverbs 16:9 (NASB)
⁹ The mind of man plans his way,
But the Lord directs his steps.

Chapter 3
The First Hunt

One of the magical elements in life is that great journeys can unfold in the most unexpected places.

April 3, 1999

As they lined up along the sidewalk, the residents of the nursing home awaited the children's arrival. Tim's grandmother, Grandma Nita, was in the front row. I am sure she had been looking forward to this day for quite some time. She wore her favorite red sweater. She had applied her makeup down to her bright red lipstick.

The beautiful blue sky set the tone for a gorgeous spring day. It was Easter weekend and the promise of a new beginning was clear in the blooming trees and flowers that covered the landscape. Out across the lawn, it looked as though someone had spread glitter. Easter eggs were glistening in the sun's rays and gave a magical appearance to the ground. The children anxiously peered out at all the treasures. The smell of Easter flowers filled the air.

Grandma Nita smiled proudly from her chair under the awning. Her eyes glistened with joy as we approached her. We gave many hugs and then turned our attention to the lawn, which sparkled with the glow of Easter treasures. With Caitlynn not walking yet, I held her and Courtney took part in the Easter egg hunt.

The hunt drew to an end as the children cleared the lawn of its treasures. Tim and his buddy, Doug, started a conversation up about the upcoming turkey season.

Doug excitedly mentioned to Tim that he should try turkey hunting. The enthusiasm in his voice sparked Tim's curiosity. As they continued to talk, they set up plans to go scouting and planned to hunt opening weekend together.

At the very moment they made those plans on Easter weekend 1999, the trajectory of our lives changed forever. Both Doug and Tim were unaware that a journey began, a journey that would still be going strong 25 years later.

To think Tim has not turkey hunted from his youth is a crazy thought. With his depth of passion and the degree to which it has engulfed our lives in many aspects, you would have thought that he has been doing it since he was a young child. While he did fish and hunt deer and other small game with his dad and uncles, he didn't start turkey hunting until his late 20s. He has always been passionate about the outdoors. He harvested his first deer at age 12 on an archery hunt, his first hunt in a stand by himself.

After going on his first turkey hunt, Tim was hooked. He quickly became addicted. With turkey hunting, there is a very intriguing connection between the hunter and bird. Through communication, the hunt ensues. As he became successful and took his first turkey, he learned more about the hunt. He gained such a passion for the hunt he wanted to continue to learn more and more about it.

In 2003, he decided he was going to get a lathe and try his hand at making his own pot call to hunt with. He thought it would be great to create a call himself, call a turkey in and harvest that turkey. I knew at this point his passion for turkey hunting ran deep. He was hooked.

He was talking to his good friend, Robbie, about getting a lathe and mentioned his desire to make a turkey call to take turkey hunting. Robbie said he thought his dad might have a lathe that he was no longer using and he would check to see if he would be interested in selling it.

This indeed was true, and Tim was very excited. He picked up the lathe. To our surprise, we discovered the lathe was on a very nice table. Inside the drawers were all the turning tools he would need to begin his work. Tim purchased this lathe for $100. We never would have guessed that this lathe would be the beginning of a lifelong trade of turkey call making. Tim still uses this lathe today, over 20 years later.

While he has added many pieces of equipment and tools, this lathe is an important part of his workshop. His shop is in our garage, a garage that I am pretty sure has never contained a vehicle. The memories made in this shop are much too many to count. Many masterpieces have begun their journey to fruition in this very shop. Once the idea begins its great journey from Tim's mind and into existence, it is this very shop where it comes to life.

I often wonder what would have happened if, at that beautiful Easter egg hunt in 1999, Doug would not have mentioned to Tim about going on that first turkey hunt. Since the moment he tried turkey hunting, his life has veered in one direction.

It was at that very moment that our wonderful journey began. I smile when I think back to that day and the journey we have been on since then. Little did we know that very decision would change our lives forever, in ways we could never have imagined.

The friendships we have made along the way are such a blessing. Little did we know how far this passion would take us. A passion I am sure will last a lifetime.

25 years and counting.

Chapter 4
A Family Affair

As I opened my eyes, the sunrise glimmered through the window. As I familiarized myself and awakened my senses, the wonderful feeling of relaxation filled my heart. I glanced across the camper. I saw the girls each snuggly wrapped in their sleeping bags. Last night was a much quieter night than our first night here. The terrible storms had made for quite a traumatizing escapade. We had to break camp at 2:00 a.m. and sleep in the truck's cab. Not knowing the area fully, we were afraid to travel too far in the night's darkness. We learned quickly that the storms here in Oklahoma are not like our storms at home in Indiana. They seem so much larger, much more ominous. You can spot them from miles away as they approach.

Tim had left before daylight to try his hand at the Rio Grande wild turkey. After much research, we had chosen the Black Kettle National Grasslands as his public land hunting spot for this trip to Oklahoma.

As I slowly arose, I slipped outside to catch a view of the gorgeous sunrise. The feeling of exiting the camper and entering an entirely new world was one I will always cherish. In an unfamiliar location, everything is foreign to your senses. The feeling of the air, the smells and even the sounds are new.

The view of Skipout Lake from our campsite was absolutely gorgeous. The blue sky and fluffy clouds seemed to touch the horizon.

As the sun rose, the sparkle on the lake painted a gorgeous picture for my eyes to see. The excitement of starting the day with an adventure filled me.

I couldn't wait to hear the stories about Tim's hunt. Successful or not, I knew he would enjoy his time hunting.

As I sat outside enjoying the view, I heard rustling in the camper. I knew the girls had finally awakened. I was sure the excitement of an upcoming adventure had filled their thoughts as well.

As the camper door opened, the excitement in their sleepy eyes was clear. With them being 10 and 6, they were ready for a fun-filled day of adventure. We had planned an early morning walk around the lake before dad arrived back from his hunt.

"Good morning," I said, as I smiled in anticipation of their excitement.

"Good morning," they both hollered.

"Are we going on an adventure?" Courtney asked.

They could barely contain their smiles. In their hands, they held their journals. In these journals, they had documented anything that they would like to see on this trip, and in another section, they wrote of their findings and the special things they saw.

I went back into the camper to get some warmer clothes on, as the wind was quite brisk coming across the lake. Just as I found my jacket, I heard some hollering outside the camper. It scared me.

As I opened the door, Courtney was bent over beside the camper, hollering at Caitlynn, who had climbed up onto a concrete barrier.

As I stepped out, Courtney yelled, "Mom, a kangaroo rat!"

A feeling of fear overtook me. What did she say, a rat?

"I had it on my list to find and there is one under the camper," she excitedly yelled.

Just as I stepped down onto the ground, out from under the camper ran a rodent. It looked like a small mouse with a long tail and it hopped quickly along, trying to find a place to hide.

Courtney was beside herself with excitement. She had found an animal on her list.

That little kangaroo rat did not know it had just made the dreams of two girls come true. It had sparked a passion in all of us that would never leave our memory. What we had witnessed that morning was a wonderful connection with nature. It was the beginning of many great journeys. It sparked a passion that still lives in each of us today.

This is one of the many stories we have of the trips we would take. Once Tim began his journey into the turkey hunting world, we would take family/turkey hunting trips all over the United States. Tim would turkey hunt public lands and work on getting what we called his "Poor Man's Grand Slam."

Looking back on it now, there was nothing "poor" about it. It was an absolute blessing from which many memories came.

These trips together as a family strengthened us and our connection with nature. Our primary goal was to immerse the girls in the world of the outdoors and the world of turkey hunting.

During our trip to Oklahoma, staying in our pop-up camper, we explored the Black Kettle National Grasslands and an area near Elk City, Oklahoma. Tim hunted these areas and successfully took three Rio Grande turkeys.

We traveled to South Dakota and Wyoming and stayed in a cabin in the Black Hills. While there, Tim successfully harvested two Merriam wild turkeys.

On a trip to Florida, we stayed in our pop-up camper in the Green Swamp Management Area and even made a trip to Disney World. The hunting part of the trip ended unsuccessfully.

Because of the lack of success on our first trip to Florida, we made a second trip. It was on this trip to Punta Gorda that we visited Fort Myers' beach and enjoyed the sun and sand.

Tim successfully harvested an Osceola wild turkey.

During our out of state trips, the girls and I would explore and enjoy our time outdoors. Before these trips, we would have the girls research animals and other things that interested them about each place we were going. They would have a list of animals and sights they wanted to see. While we were on the trips, they would write in their journals and draw pictures of the things they saw and the experiences they had while we were on our adventure.

Many times during these adventures, they would bring to our attention the name of a particular animal that we would see or a particular element of nature that they had studied. The kangaroo rat was one of the great experiences we had encountered. They documented everything in their journals.

Once we returned from our trip, they would take the journals to school. They would share their experiences with their classmates so that they too could learn about what nature offers, especially for those children who were not familiar with it.

The trips we made were a family affair. The places we traveled, the wonderful sights we saw and the amazing time spent together as a family definitely enriched our lives. We had a wonderful time as we taught the girls about the different areas of the country and about many of the creatures that live in those areas.

We made memories to last a lifetime and allowed our roots to grow even deeper in our connection with nature and the earth.

With all our adventures, we hoped that what we would instill in our girls would carry on to our grandchildren.

There is a connection between everything in life. As we ponder on our wonderful journey, we realize just how true that is.

John Muir, one of the most-influential naturalist/explorer in the United States, said it best when he said, ***"In every walk with nature one receives far more than he seeks."***

Chapter 5
The Breakfast Meeting

As I sit and reminisce, my heart becomes full. Some things in our journey become monumental when we look back on them. At the time that they occur, they are important special events. However, when you look back on them after years have passed, their role in the journey becomes much more significant. They become part of a grand scheme.

As I think back to one of those moments in our journey, I rewind my thoughts back to February 2004, during the time of the 28th Annual National Wild Turkey Federation's convention. This year, they held the convention at the Columbus Convention Center in Columbus, Ohio.

At this time, Earl Mickel was writing his third book, "Long Beards, Callmakers and Memories." Earl was a collector of turkey calls. His collection of calls from call makers all over was one of the largest. He was a great turkey hunter and enjoyed learning about call makers and their call making journey. He had contacted Tim prior to this event, as he wanted to interview him to be in his book.

Tim and I, along with our oldest daughter Courtney, planned a breakfast meeting during the convention in Columbus. We were to meet with Earl and a good friend of his, Ralph Snodgrass.

When we arrived at breakfast, Earl and Ralph were sitting in the booth. We slid in nervously. This was a big deal for us, and our excitement was undeniable.

Earl was a very jovial man. When he told us about his goal, it was very apparent that he was very passionate about his books.

Ralph was a friendly man whom you could easily carry on conversation with.

Between the two of them, our nervousness quickly abated.

As Earl interviewed Tim, he asked him several questions about his journey with call making and what his plans for call making were.

We had a wonderful breakfast and truly enjoyed meeting the two of them.

I remember Earl asking Tim one very important question. A question that he answered, not knowing what the future held. It was a question that definitely, in looking back, defined our journey.

He asked, "Tim, what do you plan on doing with your call making in the future?"

He added, "Will you mass produce your calls, or will you custom make them?"

That day, with Tim's answer, he would continue his journey in the custom call making realm. He would continue to produce his calls one at a time.

Little did we know the course of events that would occur over the next 19 years. The events that we could not have imagined in our wildest dreams.

Tim has kept his strict beliefs in custom making each call. The call must first sound great. There is no deviation from that very important factor. Then he will add his beautiful artwork to add uniqueness and his own personal touch. He enjoys creating a call to the customer's specifications. A call that sounds amazing for the turkey woods and one that is beautiful, as well. He hopes to create an heirloom to be enjoyed for years to come.

Fast forward 19 years from that breakfast interview, we met back up with Ralph "Snozz" Snodgrass during Unicoi 2023. We reminisced about the wonderful memories of that breakfast meeting. Reflecting on our 19-year journey was very inspiring for Tim and me.

As we talked, Ralph said, "Tim, Earl would be proud!"

His words echoed through our hearts and we will joyfully carry them along through our journey as cherished memories.

It is monumental moments such as this that pave the path for our journey. The moments that carry us through to the future.

Chapter 6
Morels & Memories
Carrying on a Tradition

Life is full of lessons. Each lesson we learn has a direct connection to our future journey. Every one gives us a deeper understanding of life itself.

Tim learned a hard lesson as our oldest daughter, Courtney, came of age to hunt. It brought him so much excitement to take her out into the woods. He had always wished to have a son or daughter to teach all that he knew about his passion for hunting. He yearned to carry on the traditions he learned as a child and make new traditions for his children. Through no intentional fault of his own, he instinctually wanted her to experience hunting. With too much enthusiasm and speed, he dove right into teaching her. Through all of this came an unforeseen problem; she was afraid of shooting a gun. Being the avid hunter that Tim is, he just assumed that it was a normal process, one of which she had to overcome. He decided that the only way to overcome a fear such as this is to practice.

After much anguish for both of them, there was an arrival to the conclusion that shooting a gun was not something she would overcome.

It was a painful realization for Tim. He expressed his feelings of failure. He felt he had ruined his opportunity to teach her his passion. I felt a great deal of sadness about his situation.

In retrospect, to the sadness, I felt a great sense of relief from Courtney when she convinced her dad that it would not happen. I am sure that the feelings of letting him down weighed heavy on her heart.

It took some time for Tim to accept the situation. However, once he understood, this part of our journey evolved.

Now, whether it was any fault of Tim, or whether it was just not in the plan for Courtney to be a hunter, he took responsibility for it. In all actuality, maybe she was just not meant to be a hunter? We later realized that God had other plans for her to be an outdoor enthusiast and not partake in hunting.

Tim and Courtney enjoyed time together in the outdoors, engaging in activities such as hiking, fishing, antler shed hunting, and morel mushroom hunting in the spring. She immediately gained a passion for these activities.

She especially loved hunting for morels. For her, there was something wonderful about meandering through the woods in the early spring, searching for these little treasures.

Spring is a time when the woods come alive. The plants and trees are awakening from their long winter nap. It is a time of rejuvenation for all of God's creation. I believe all of us feel a renewal in the spring after we have gone through the long, cold winter. There is something about it that rejuvenates our soul. The breathing in of the cool spring air and the warm sunshine shining through the canopy of the trees all play a part in this renewal. There is a casting of the sunlight on all the jewels emerging from the brown leaves on the ground, as if a stage light was lighting up the stage for God's greatest creations. It is our time in the woods during this time of the year that all our senses are aware of this grand renewing. Even the smell of the moist soil in the air is one that rekindles our soul.

The reward for finding a small patch of morels popping up through the brown leaves is so exciting. As hunters, we know that if we find one; we are likely to find more. Once we have been hunting for a while, our eyes become accustomed to seeing them, as we know just where to look. We perfect our skills with each one that we find.

As we search, our childhood memories of Easter egg hunting come back to us, and we feel the same excitement we would have with each egg we found. We rekindle with our childhood.

Even after Courtney gave birth to our first sweet grandson, Kawhi, she would pack him up on the front of her chest in his carrier and take him on the wonderful journeys with Tim to search for morels. They would teach him all about their passion for hunting these mushrooms. Even at 15 months old, he would come back excited and rejuvenated after their adventure. He seemed to experience the profound rejuvenation that resulted from venturing into the woods. The serenity and all that it held did his young soul a great deal of good.

They would come back with many stories to tell. Stories of Kawhi finding a morel or two as he learned the skill of maneuvering around in the woods. Stories of the box turtles they would see wondering aimlessly through the vast woods in search of their perfect mate. There would almost always be a story of a gobbling turkey they heard, a group of turkeys they saw, or the occasional whitetail deer sighting.

Because of the exact steps of our journey, even though they did not turn out as we had planned, we now have grandsons who get out in nature daily. They hike, explore, and enjoy God's creation. Their number one choice at the ages five and one is to be outside exploring, learning and taking it all in.

Our journey may not have gone according to plan, but the result was filled with hope. Perhaps Tim needed to learn this lesson before being blessed with three precious grandsons. The will to continue to show our children all that nature offers, even in the presence of perceived failure, planted that seed for our future grandsons.

To accomplish great things, we must only have the will to succeed and succeed we shall.

Chapter 7
The Gift of Life

In the spring, all in nature is new. It is a time for new beginnings. The reemergence of plants and trees, as they wake from their winter nap. The days become warmer and longer. We all experience a sort of rejuvenation. For those of us one with nature, we enjoy being outside and seeing the world as mother nature awakens the earth. The once barren flower beds became alive with a kaleidoscope of vibrant flowers, their delicate fragrance floating in the warm breeze. Being outside is our happy place. It is a place that is very familiar to us, a place where we feel whole.

I am a gardener down into my soul. I love getting my hands into the earth and working the soil. Every year, I plant seeds and watch them as they grow from their tiny existence into a beautiful plant. I love nurturing the plants to where they provide us with an abundance of fruits and vegetables. This has been a great pleasure of mine for as long as I can remember.

It was a warm spring day in May 2019. Tim and I were enjoying our usual outdoor activities of working in the yard. Turkey season had ended for us, and we were catching up on yard work.

While turkey season is in, we are very busy with hunting and we get behind on our chores. Our focus is narrow when the season is in and we focus solely on the wild turkey.

The sunshine was beaming down with its golden glow and its warm touch on our skin. This time of the year is always such a warm welcome to us after a long, cold winter. Our post-turkey season ritual was in full swing. As Tim did the trimming with the weed eater, I was attempting to push mow the yard. I was more than eager and, as crazy as it sounds, excited to be outside doing it.

My thoughts lingered around the excitement and accomplishment of tidying up the yard by cutting the grass.

However, on this day, as I mowed the yard, I noticed a tightness in my chest. There was a very uncomfortable feeling of fatigue. My breath was very hard to get control of and the fear that it would go away completely was looming around my every thought. I could not proceed for over five or ten minutes. I would become increasingly short of breath and had to sit down for a bit. This went on for a while, and I became frustrated.

Tim, noticing my odd behavior, asked me what was wrong. When I told him, he said, "You've been doing a lot this weekend, you're just wore out from all of that."

He said, "Let me finish and you go sit down and take it easy."

A feeling of frustration overtook me, and I agreed to take his advice. I willingly convinced myself that I had indeed done a lot of work and was probably just wore out from it all.

As my work week began that Tuesday morning, I struggled to make it up the long walk I had to get up to my office. I was short of breath. I felt an unusually "uncomfortable" feeling.

As this continued a couple of more days, my mind tried to justify it by thinking that I was just wore out from the weekend.

By Thursday morning, I had to stop several times and rest on my way up the walk. This concerned me. Being a transcriptionist in a cardiology office, I know all too well that these symptoms are not normal. I knew they could be dangerous, and I decided I would go talk to one of the nurse practitioners that work in the office with me. His office was down the hall from mine.

As I walked down the hallway, I had the extreme urge to sit down. A very uncomfortable and unfamiliar feeling overtook my body.

By the time I made it to his office, I was extremely short of breath and had to sit down. Fear filled my mind, and I could not think clearly. I could tell by the look on his face that he was concerned as well.

He immediately requested that I go for a battery of tests.

It wasn't until he told me, "I think you need to get your husband here as soon as possible," that my world changed. My mind reeled from those simple words.

All I could muster from the depths of myself, as I made my phone call to Tim, was, "You need to get here as soon as possible. Something is wrong!"

The crackling of his voice scared me even more.

He assured me, "I'll be right there."

I felt scared about what was happening inside my body. Having experienced nothing like this before, fear overwhelmed me beyond what I knew was even possible.

Tim arrived at the office in record time. They put me in a wheelchair and organized transportation to the hospital for testing, and later they transferred me to the Emergency Department for admission.

The testing that I underwent was very familiar to me from my work aspect, but I had never actually had the testing myself. I had a whole new perspective on what patients are feeling when they have their testing. The testing that I type about every day.

My test results did not come back encouraging. I had many things going on in my body. There were life-threatening issues I was not even aware of.

My testing showed that I had pulmonary embolisms in both lungs, almost completely saddled across the top.

I, unknowingly, had deep venous thromboses in both legs and, at some point, they had broken loose and caused the embolisms in my lungs.

My health had taken center stage in my life. I had never prayed so much for my next breath to be taken. My breathing became a conscious action. No longer did it linger in my subconscious mind as it had before. Fear overtook my body. The feeling was one of great battle. I was going to fight. It was my only option. What if the next breath was not there? I was not ready to die. I had a journey to make. Little did I know that this was a part of that journey. A part of the journey that would lead me to a greater appreciation of life.

The Ekosonic Endovascular System (EKOS) procedure and my stay in the ICU Unit were the scariest times of my life. EKOS was the treatment of choice for my situation. They administered an IV line into my neck. This line pumped heparin and some other fluids into my body. The medical team connected me to a gigantic machine during this procedure, which lasted just under 24 hours. It used ultrasonic sound waves to break up the clots in my lungs. My fear of that machine and what it was or was not doing to my body was astounding.

The weeks and months following that day were scary and extremely challenging for me. It was unlike any other challenge I had been through. The testing, procedures, hospitalizations, surgeries, and recovery were all grueling.

After having gone through a trauma such as this, the fear of it happening again is always lingering in the dark shadows of my mind. I am hypersensitive to any unfamiliar feelings that I have. To this day, I continue to work on this struggle.

The one thing that I know for sure is that Tim was by my side the entire time, encouraging me and giving me the hope I needed to get through. I will forever be grateful to him. He has been with me through my darkest times. He was that beacon of light shining when my light was fading.

It takes a while for the things we endure to process through our minds. Over time, our minds process them and create a memory. This is our own interpretation of the experience.

That day in May, I changed. My outlook on life changed. This experience made me look at my life and focus on the parts that are the most important. Through this, I have become more grateful for my life.

A quote from Wayne Dyer says it all for me, *"Stop acting as if life is a rehearsal. Live this day as if it were your last. The past is over and gone. The future is not guaranteed."*

I will always remember that life is a precious gift. We must enjoy it to the fullest, as we are not promised tomorrow.

Isaiah 41:10 (NASB)
10 Do not fear, for I am with you;
Do not anxiously look about you, for I am your God.
I will strengthen you, surely I will help you,
Surely I will uphold you with My righteous right hand.

Chapter 8
Being One With Nature

As I recovered from my illness, my breath continued to normalize. Through my journey, I gained a deeper appreciation for every breath I take. I look at life differently and with a greater respect. It is with that respect that my next visit to the woods was a completely unique experience.

With this profound respect and new experience, I must ask the following questions.

Have you ever been in the woods before it awakens?

Have you rested your mind in the darkness, awaiting a great journey with the first light of day?

While many of the inhabitants of the woods are still sleeping, there is a calmness. A feeling of tranquility comes to us in the silence before dawn. A time when you can clear your mind to the fullest. This is a time I believe we all should experience, at least once.

As your eyes cannot see and your ears only hear the faint sounds of crickets and frogs whistling in the darkness, you feel a serenity unlike any other you have felt before. Your breathing is shallow and your mind is calm. It is as if you are waiting in the shadows, waiting for the woods to awaken. Your eyes and ears play tricks on you. Was that a movement in the distance? Was that a sound of leaves rustling? Is something approaching me?

As you rest your body in the darkness, an ever-so-subtle brightening occurs. As the light intensifies, you gain your senses a little better. It becomes easier to see your surroundings. You can feel the coldness of the dew falling gently onto the leaves.

Suddenly, the sound of the first bird awakening fills the air, as if a choir were singing. There is something magical to be felt as nature's creatures awaken. You cannot help but feel happy when you hear the joyous song fill your ears. Many others join the serenade as they proclaim their delight in the rising sun. The glow of the sunrise slowly fills your once-dark world with light. The sounds overwhelm your mind. You try to focus on each one as if you could hear what they are saying.

In the middle of your thoughts and focus, as if a bolt of lightning strikes, you hear the unmistakable sound of a wild turkey gobbling. This sound completely engulfs your once-focused mind. Instantly, you remember why you are there in the woods. You are then suddenly pushed back into your hunting mode and you realize that your ability to become one with the woods is of the utmost importance. You must step up your skills, as you are after a wild turkey and the wild turkey knows his way in the woods. Your mind races with excitement as your adrenaline amps up. It is almost too much to bear. Every move you make will be critical as you begin your chess game with the ol' wary gobbler. The sounds you make will affect the outcome of your hunt. You will face a test. The only thing that is guaranteed with your test, if you are unsuccessful in your hunt, is that you will learn a little more about that gobbler than you knew before.

For me, it is truly more than just a turkey hunt. It is a time for my mind to rest, a time for reflection, and a time for making sense of the thoughts of life that fill my mind. It is a time of problem solving and deep thought. Our minds can truly be a peace when we are amongst nature. Our bodies become grounded. We gain a certain clarity that we cannot get anywhere else. It is a clarity that allows us to relax and feel freedom from our everyday situations.

In the beginning, a hunter must get their positioning figured out, a knowledge of where the gobbler is. This can sometimes prove to be very challenging. Once you figure out your position, the hunt quickly turns into an exciting journey. Each time you hear the gobble, you have a better understanding of the hunt. However, hearing a gobble is not always the case. As all hunters know, many times the turkeys will be silent. They will not give us the slightest idea of where they are or what their next move will be. It is at these times where we must rely on our instinct to guide us. In times of silence, it becomes a battle between our instincts and the instinct of the mighty wild turkey. Patience is a virtue in this battle.

I enjoy seeing the things in nature that you do not see unless you get out and find them. There are many sounds and sights to be enjoyed in the woods. The sound of the first bird waking up after a night of silence, the sound of trickling water from a stream as it makes its way through the woods floor and the scurrying around of God's creatures. It is the soft moss on the trees and the woodland plants as they awaken from their winter nap and rise toward the sun.

There are many creatures that I enjoy seeing as well. The box turtles as they make their journey to find their perfect mate. The squirrels as they scamper through the trees. Their sounds echo through the woods. If they see you, they will most certainly try to alert the other creatures of your location. There is nothing worse than having a disgruntled squirrel give away your location as you try to hunt an old wary gobbler. The screeching of a Blue Jay or a crow will also certainly prove to give your hidden location away. There is also the feel of the cool ground as you sit against a tree and try to blend in with the beauty surrounding you.

It is such an enjoyable time that many times I forget why I am there. However, I am quickly reminded of my purpose there when I once again hear that thunderous gobble sounding off. It is then that I am directed back to that chess game, as I anxiously decide what my next move will be.

"Look deep into nature, and then you will understand everything better." – **Albert Einstein**

Chapter 9
Mother's Love

It is nearly impossible to concentrate on oneself when a loved one's life is at stake. This was certainly the case with Tim after my illness. As my recovery progressed through the summer, our lives normalized. The time neared when Tim would begin his piece for the National Wild Turkey Federation's Custom Callmaking competition. With my illness having taken a toll on both of us, he appeared to be lacking enthusiasm to get out into his shop.

It was a beautiful morning. Tim and I had gotten our cups of coffee and we began our ritual of sitting on the loveseat watching the birds as they enjoy their morning breakfast outside our window.

On our porch stood two concrete bird baths and a table with bird seed scattered across it. A variety of birds would visit us daily. The cardinals were especially active. There were several nesting in the area, and we watched as the parents cared for their baby fledglings.

It was mid-summer and my flower beds were in full bloom. The daylilies put on a show for us. Red, pink, yellow, and orange flowers filled the yard with color. The clematis which climbed its way up the side of Tim's shop was showing off its beautiful purple flowers. Bird houses, made by Tim, decorated our front yard. It is our little piece of heaven on earth.

As he sat staring off into space, I asked, "What are you thinking about?"

The lack of enthusiasm in his eyes scared me.

He whispered, "Nothing".

I knew that was not true. Having known him all these years, something was bothering him. It was crucial to revive his enthusiasm, and my heart was steadfast in its determination to make it happen. His internal alarms should have been going off. It was time for him to get a project started, but something was holding him back.

I asked, "Are you going to do a piece for the convention this next year?"

He shrugged his shoulders. I had never seen him like this and I knew I needed to help him get his motivation back.

I told him, "You know, I am feeling much better."

That got his attention.

"I really want you to do a piece for the convention," I said.

As we continued to discuss it, a smile formed across his face. A wave of satisfaction washed over me, as I knew I had effectively gotten that message across.

He smiled again and said, "I already have a great idea, one that will be very meaningful." At the point we were in on our journey, I knew it would be a heartfelt piece.

As he explained the piece to me, I tried my best to understand his theory behind it. I lacked the type of artistic mind that I needed to understand.

I was thankful that I could get through to him and explain my feelings.

From that moment on, he immersed himself in the project. He was putting his heart and soul into it. He would get up early in the morning before he left for work and he would begin work again on it once he arrived home from work in the evening.

This was a very necessary step in recovery for both of us. It is what we needed to get our lives back to an even more normal state.

"Mother's Love" was the name of the beautiful piece he created. A wonderful story was told in this piece. It was a piece that included a hen protecting her poults under her wing. It told a story of the hen's undying love for her poults.

In Tim's eyes, that piece was a portrayal of my love for my family. Gratefulness washed over us, a warm and comforting embrace, as we acknowledged the journey we were undertaking.

Little did we know of the journey that was ahead of us. We had been through so much. We did not know what was about to take place. Within the next year, our lives would take another drastic turn. A turn that we never saw coming. The unimaginable would yet again happen. What would we do? How would our journey change?

The next chapter in our journey would make us even more grateful and appreciative of life.

Chapter 10
The Easter Bird

In our house, the anticipation of turkey season is an exciting time. It is in resemblance to Christmas. There is much discussion and planning that goes into turkey season. This discussion and planning can occur as early as many months before the season arrives. Tim has told us we will always have an opportunity for him to take us hunting, if we choose to go. I am very grateful for this opportunity, as I have yet to go on a successful hunt by myself and have only been hunting twice alone.

Tim will always evaluate which of us wants to hunt and, even though he would not admit to it, he also would prefer to know what our level of determination will be for the hunts in question. I always laugh inside when he asks the questions. It is as if he is checking on what his excitement level will be, depending on how much hunting he is going to do. His preference would be for all of us to have the desire to hunt. This situation would exponentially increase his days in the field hunting. You see, he considers it hunting whether he is the hunter or if it is one of us doing the hunting.

As I am sure many hunters can attest, the anticipation of the season to open is an exciting time. During this time, there is much to be done. A hunter needs to take an inventory of his supplies, his calls, his camo and his gun. The hunter must check all the gear to ensure it is in usable form. This would always manifest into a grand pre-season ritual. I truly believe this is a way for the hunter to extend his season, in this sport that truly seems to be a brief season that quickly ends. Embracing the spirit of turkey season, hunters carefully devise plans and eagerly embrace every chance to prolong the season by inviting more hunters or venturing into new hunting territories, arranging everything meticulously. The planning and preparing is a way to direct the mind and calm the overwhelming excitement that inevitably takes over a hunter as soon as spring begins. The temperature, the feeling outside and even the smell can awaken the senses of the internal clock of the hunter and throw them into a familiar excitement.

Around our house, turkey sounds are a daily occurrence. There is always a call to be played and tested, whether it is a call being tuned for a customer or a call being practiced for the anticipation of turkey season. This is a sound that I am familiar with and hear regularly. It is such a common occurrence that our male cockatiel can perfectly mimic a hen turkey. It is a hilarious sound to hear. When I think about it, he has been hearing these sounds for the entire time that we have had him, which is over 15 years.

In March 2012, Caitlynn was excited to hunt the Kentucky youth season. It is a great opportunity for youth, 16 and under, to hunt a weekend without having the adult hunters in the woods hunting. This year, she was 13 years old. Tim was very excited that she had such a great desire to hunt the youth season. In his description of her, he always says, "She is my killer!" This statement to him had the meaning that she was a skilled hunter and a successful one at that. He would say it with the utmost respect for the wild turkey and hunting itself. He has taught me and his girls that very respect.

He made plans for the youth hunt. Tim eagerly anticipated the return to the public land in Kentucky for this hunt. This spot also had great camping possibilities, so I went with them. We would set up our pop-up camper and have an enjoyable and relaxing weekend, with them doing as much hunting as they could. I looked forward to this trip, as it allowed me to get away from my usual duties of cleaning the house and laundry. It was always a very relaxing time for me. Having the ability to be right there when they return from their hunt was also a significant advantage. I didn't have to hear about their adventure over the phone as they were driving back home.

With the youth season falling on Easter weekend, we decided to head back home Sunday morning after their hunt. This would allow us to join in on the Easter festivities that were planned with family. Courtney was working this weekend, so it would just be Tim, myself, Caitlynn and our 5-year-old miniature dachshund, Jake.

April 7, 2012

The Saturday Hunt

Early in the morning hours, they located and set up on a gobbling turkey. Traveling in under the cover of darkness, they could position themselves in tight on this bird. With the rising of the sun, Tim began to tree yelp to get the attention of the gobbler. It wasn't long after that the excitement turned into disappointment after realizing that to their left there was another hunter coming in with a youth to set up on the same bird.

With realizing the situation, Tim had to do something that he never liked to do.

He whispered to Caitlynn, "We need to back out of here because this could be an unsafe situation."

The disappointment that he witnessed come across her face was that of which he would not forget. He knew how hard she had worked for that very moment and how patient she had been. To back out from the situation was not a simple task, but necessary for their safety.

The rest of the day, they burned their boots with the miles they covered. They searched high and low for another gobbler with no luck.

April 8, 2012—Easter

The Sunday Hunt

After the unsuccessful hunt on Saturday, Tim and Caitlynn headed out into the darkness bright and early on Sunday morning. Just outside the camper, I could hear them discussing their morning plan as they put on their boots. They still spoke with as much excitement in their voices as they had when we arrived on Friday night. Hope remained for a successful hunt and they eagerly anticipated it. I could hear their voices slowly diminish as they headed out into the darkness. I felt their excitement deep inside me as I remember the excitement felt when I headed out on a hunt myself. No doubt, they had a well-executed plan and would only deviate if necessary.

The plan this morning was to head to a lush green field they had found on their journey the day before. Unfortunately, the birds they encountered were with hens. Tim tried everything he knew. The birds were not cooperating.

As they watched these birds for hours on this field, their time slowly ticked away. We had made plans for Easter and they had a deadline to return to camp in order to make the Easter festivities.

While walking back to camp, Caitlynn felt frustrated because they had to abandon turkeys twice.

Tim tried to explain to her that this was just part of hunting and that it does not always work out the way you want it to.

Upon their arrival back, they once again explained their misfortune. I could see the disappointment on Caitlynn's face.

As Tim explained to her that with those birds, it was just a "waiting game" and their time had run out.

At that very moment, a switch flipped in her mind.

In an instant, she grabbed Tim's vest and her gun, on her own, and walked down the road bed they had just came from.

Tim said, "Caitlynn, what are you doing?"

She hollered back at him, "I want a bird."

At that very moment, Tim realized she had that gritty desire that he himself had. That endless determination that he had inside him was inside her as well. It was as if he was looking at himself.

As he convinced her to come back, the discussion ensued about Caitlynn contacting her sister to see if it was okay for us to arrive later in the day for the Easter celebration. She agreed and made the phone call.

As she hung up the phone, a smile made its way to her face. That same smile I had seen on her face before they headed out on that first hunt Saturday morning was back, and this time it included an even more intense determination to harvest a wild turkey.

As I watched them walk off in the distance, I knew their plans were to head back to the lush green field.

As they approached the field, Tim scanned it and could not find the birds. He knew they were not far, so they got into position closer to where they had seen the birds that morning. He put a hen decoy out in the field and they tucked in against an old tree on the hillside.

He called every so often.

After about an hour, the same group of birds came out into the field. They were not initially interested in any of his calling. It started out as a replay of their earlier hunt.

As they remained persistent, suddenly it was as if fate changed its course. Tim noticed that two of the birds showed an interest in his calling. As if it was meant to be, they broke away from the group and headed toward their set up.

In his mind, Tim knew if the script played out, this could be the situation they had hoped for. He knew that her persistence and determination were about to pay off.

As the situation played out, Tim could not believe what was happening.

As the birds got closer, he said, "Once they are at the decoy, they are within range. When you are comfortable, you can shoot."

Caitlynn did not waste a second once they arrived at the decoy.

She said, "I can see him in the scope, dad."

Back at camp, I heard a shot from the direction they had left. Excitement filled my body as I jumped up and headed out of the camper. I anxiously awaited their arrival, hoping there was a successful hunt.

As I saw them approaching from a distance, I saw Caitlynn with a turkey over her shoulder. As they got closer, I saw the smile on her face that lit up the day. Her patience and persistence had paid off.

The well-deserved Easter Bird had been harvested.

Chapter 11

The Prom Objective

Reminiscent of the swelling winds of a great hurricane, sometimes life carries us in an unexpected direction. A direction that surprises us. With a firm hold, it leads us on a journey beyond imagination. It will intensify our senses and overall substantiate the fact that anything is possible. It is up to our imagination and our will to accomplish our goals.

April 18, 2015

As I think back to the many wonders of being the mom of two daughters, I can't help but think of the excitement I carried, as I found out with each pregnancy that I was having a girl. As many times, I believe that mothers secretly, and sometimes not so secretly, have a desire to have a daughter. A daughter to share common interests and to later in life have a best friend, someone as close to oneself as possible. Being the mother of a daughter holds many joyous moments. My memory takes me back to an abounding amount of soft, pink dresses, precious pastel outfits and many hair bows and ribbons. Oh, the joys of being the mother of daughters. As they grow up, the connection between mother and daughter is like no other. From the time they are born, until they become mothers themselves, life is sweet having girls.

Naturally, with our outdoor loving lifestyle, our girls were very much lovers of the outdoors and all of God's creations. From the time they were small, they loved spending their days soaking up the warm rays of the sun and exploring nature's bounty. Often, as a family, we enjoyed days spent outdoors. From journeys into the woods near our home to trips taken to places never visited before, we submerged ourselves in the exploration of all that nature offers.

Even with our youngest daughter Caitlynn loving to hunt with Tim, her aspirations for a particular warm spring Saturday, April 18, 2015, were a surprise to both of us.

It was the weekend prior to this special day that Caitlynn had been talking with Tim about a goal she had wanted to accomplish. This goal was not your everyday goal for a 16-year-old girl.

I had overheard Caitlynn discussing with Tim in a very confident voice. She said, "Dad, next weekend is Prom."

Tim said, "Yes, it is!" He had been a part of the planning and was aware of our hunt for the perfect dress for her.

Undenounced to both of us, the next words out of her mouth were as unexpected as rain on a sunshiny day.

"I want to go turkey hunting on the opening day of the youth season, shoot a turkey in the morning, and take pictures with it in my prom dress," she said without hesitation.

The look on Tim's face at that moment was as if every dream he had ever wished for had come true.

He had already accepted the fact that the youth season would pass, and his girls would not experience it in the way he wished, especially with the youth season falling on the weekend of prom. It was the last year for her to hunt the youth season in Indiana.

Just as quickly as she finished speaking, Tim spoke with a great deal of excitement. As he pushed the words right out of his mouth, he exclaimed, "We can definitely do that!"

I wondered if the thought even crossed either of their minds as to the actual odds of being able to accomplish that seemingly impossible goal? You see, at that point in time, my mind worked differently than it currently does. If I would have known then what I know now, I would have thought much differently. My mind would have allowed me to think confidently about that accomplishment.

Tim has always enjoyed taking people hunting. It is a great love of his and it always has been. I can honestly say that I believe he loves taking someone hunting more than he loves being successful at a hunt himself.

Soon after their conversation, the intense planning began. It would need to be a well-orchestrated plan. With a hair appointment scheduled for Caitlynn in the early afternoon, time would be of essential importance. Filled with determination and armed with a solid plan, they exuded confidence in their ability to give their all for success.

Once they figured out all the details, the only thing left to do was to wait for the big day to arrive.

As the week progressed, their determination and planning was unmatched by any I had ever seen. The excitement built as time drew near. They both knew that to pull this off successfully would be a monumental accomplishment. One that would have a very special place in the many memories already in place.

Upon arising, they both excitedly prepared for the hunt, like small children at Christmas time, anxiously awaiting to see what Santa had brought them. The extravagant plan was gone through with a fine-tooth comb.

As they went out the door into the darkness, I reminded them of the time in which they needed to return in order to make the ever so important hair appointment. For the first time, I realized that the hair appointment, to Caitlynn, was not as exciting as it had once been. Her focus had most certainly shifted to other things, those of which her father was extremely thankful for. Off they went into the quiet darkness of the woods, like two small children on their first day of school.

As I did many times before, throughout the morning, I wondered how things were going. I tried to imagine if they had been successful in striking up a gobbler before the sun rose and filled the woods with light. In the usual fashion of my mind, I would dream of scenarios as I anxiously awaited their arrival home. I would be so excited to hear the stories of their hunt, whether they were successful or not. There was almost always a lesson or two learned in the turkey woods on every hunt. These lessons would later become stories told and precious cargo carried in our intricate minds. Locked away in a vault and never to be forgotten. They would become the glorious memories told in the future.

As the time drew closer to 11:00, I had heard nothing from them. I was much too afraid to text them to see how things were going. I clung to the adage; no news is good news! I wondered if they had been successful and, if not, I tried to imagine what was going through their minds as the time to return home drew nearer.

Just as the time was dangerously nearing time for us to leave, I heard them talking outside. With much excitement, I could barely move my feet fast enough to get outside and see what had happened.

As I cautiously entered the garage, I saw their smiling faces and felt the excitement that filled the room. It was at that point that I had my answer. It was most certainly the smiles of success. Laying on the floor next to Caitlynn was proof of the fact that she had indeed successfully completed her goal. That turkey was not just any turkey. It was one of brilliant planning and a will for accomplishment. As they were full of excitement and success, my body filled with it as well.

Once I congratulated her and the cheering quieted, they told me the exciting story of the hunt.

Just before they had decided that they better begin their unsuccessful trek back home, Caitlynn saw some movement off to her left. It was movement that Tim could not see because of his placement around the side of a tree they were sitting against.

Tim whispered, "Sis, I can't see the turkeys. Make sure you see a visible beard."

She carefully searched for a beard to confirm that she could shoot. Once she felt comfortable, she took the shot.

With Tim not able to see the events unfold, she had to set this shot up on her own. I can only imagine how anxious they both were at that moment, especially with Tim not being able to see what was happening.

As she continued to tell me the story and how it unfolded, I could feel the pride radiating from Tim and a great sense of accomplishment coming from Caitlynn. She was so proud that she could use her learned skills to create this amazingly successful hunt.

After the storytelling was done and congratulations exchanged, we hurriedly left to ensure she made it to her hair appointment.

Once her hair was complete and we arrived back home, she eloquently did her make-up and put on her dress.

At that point, it was like the transformation of a chrysalis into a butterfly. Much like in nature, the pupa goes into the form of a chrysalis and undergoes a change and then emerges as a beautiful butterfly. In the same way, Caitlynn started her day with a goal and a will to accomplish that goal. Upon completion, she emerged as a beautiful butterfly with a story to tell and her one and only Prom Turkey!

The pictures were nothing short of amazing.

When I look at these pictures, a flood of memories fills my body and brings so many feelings of love to me.

This truly was proof that all we need is the will to accomplish our goals and they will be done.

We will always remember the memories of the Prom Turkey and continue to tell the story until our days here end.

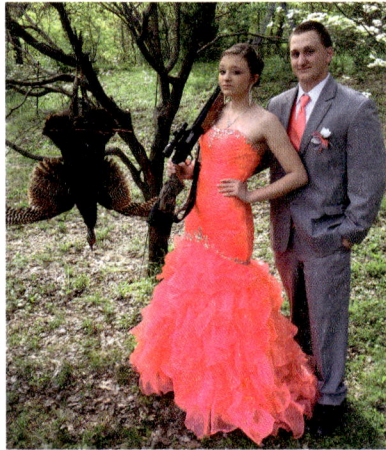

Chapter 12
With us for the Long Haul

Throughout the journey of our lives, people come and go. It is a never-ending evolution. As we start our lives, our mother, father and siblings surround us. As we grow up, we look for what really makes our heart beat. We search for those things that spark our soul. In that pursuit, we find our kindred spirits. This is "our" group of people. A group to which we connect at a much different level, sharing a like-minded interest and having a connection with the soul.

There are many gatherings, and organizations created for people who have a love for the wild turkey. During these epic gatherings, there are meetings of old friends, new friends and, most of all, enjoying the comradery with like-minded people.

These gatherings occur all over the country and each on a different scale.

There is the annual National Wild Turkey Federation (NWTF) convention in Nashville, National Wild Turkey Federation chapter banquets, and the Unicoi Callmaker's Show held in Helen, Georgia. While these are the main events Tim and I are familiar with, there are many more events as well.

In the beginning, we met people at our local NWTF banquet. This is where we started meeting the vast group of people who we call our "turkey family". This was around 2003 when Tim started making turkey calls. He would always donate a call or two to the banquet and Juniors Acquiring Knowledge, Ethics and Sportsmanship (JAKES) event. They would do a drawing and he would even do a turkey call and a hunt, guided by himself, for a lucky JAKES member.

For those of you not familiar with the NWTF, a JAKES member is a member of the organization 17 years old or younger. The organization established this program in 1981 and dedicates it to informing, educating, and involving youth in wildlife conservation and the stewardship of our natural resources.

Both of our girls, Courtney and Caitlynn, were active JAKES members and enjoyed the events held for this group.

On our journey, we have met so many wonderful people. From the beginning until now, the number of people has grown exponentially. It is amazing when we reflect. We travel to events every year to meet up with friends and share memories.

With that being said, I have a story to share with one of those wonderful people we met at the beginning of our journey. This is a gentleman we met at our local banquet and JAKES event where we would go to help raise money for the NWTF. This was one of the first places we would get together around all the people who were there supporting the same cause.

When we met Louie Bullington, he was a very active member of the local chapter of the NWTF. We joined the chapter and helped with the banquet each year. Louie was a kindred spirit. His passion for the wild turkey ran just as deep as ours.

The local chapter dissolved years ago, but we have kept in touch with Louie since that time.

You see, Louie and I have a common trait about us. We both have a fondness for water. He and I both have had adventures pertaining to bodies of water. If there is water around us during our turkey hunts or just in our time with nature, we will somehow end up wet. Louie has given me the nickname, "Mud Bug". This is a nickname that I have proven true many times.

Remembering the nickname "Mud Bug" takes me right back to another monumental moment.

As I rose to my feet, I was dripping in the muddy water. My clothes were stuck to me like tape holding the wrapping paper on a special gift.

I searched for the bag of morels that I had been so protectively holding. I felt comforted when I realized I was still clutching the bag in my hand. Searching for my phone, I found it safely nestled in my pack. Luckily, I had placed it in a plastic bag. My experiences in the outdoors had prepared me in this way.

I handed over the morel mushroom bag and my phone to Tim, as he sat there on the 4-wheeler with a look of uneasiness on his face. He was obviously waiting for my reaction and was deciding in his mind whether it was safe to laugh.

As a smile made its way onto my face, we both laughed hysterically. The release was much needed after such a stressful incident. I am not exactly sure how it happened, but somehow I ended up off the back of the 4-wheeler and into a muddy stream. I now understand and expect this type of occurrence when I encounter any type of creek or body of water in the woods, thus my nickname—"Mud Bug".

Just as my nickname has rung true many times, Louie has also proven his love for water as well.

Tim and Louie had taken a trip turkey hunting together. At one point, they came upon a rather large creek flowing out of its banks, as the season had been rainy. As Tim proceeded across a tree lying nicely over the water, Louie decided he would walk down further along the creek and cross, where the water was not deep.

Tim safely arrived on the other side. He watched Louie walk down along the creek. Once he found his shallow area to cross, he began his motion across the creek. As all hunters and nature enthusiasts know, once you are all in on your path, you go, you do not stop; you proceed forward. Well, that is just what Louie did.

As Tim watched in amazement, Louie proceeded through the creek. Less and less of him was above the water. As the water became deeper, that did not stop him. With his gun in the air, attempting to keep it dry, suddenly he was chest deep in water. He progressed on and made it to his destination on the other side of the creek. He made it safely, but certainly not even a stitch of clothing was dry. It is memories like this that will last a lifetime.

With the number of people that we have met since the very beginning of our journey, each person is special to us. They each hold a place in our heart with the memories shared.

Louie is one of those great people who has been with us for the long haul and for that friendship, we are grateful.

We meet people in unexpected places, at unexpected times, and it can even happen with a single phone call. As you will see, you never know what might happen next. Most certainly, some directions in our journey are quite unbelievable.

Chapter 13
The New York Times
November 28, 2019

With a profound feeling of defeat, I gripped the steering wheel as if it was required for any chance of accomplishment. I did it without even realizing what I was doing. When my consciousness brought me back to reality, I noticed my knuckles were white from the grip.

This feeling began as I could not find a retailer who carried the Thanksgiving Day issue of the New York Times in Evansville, the biggest town near our home. This was a whole new experience for me as, up to this point, I had never looked at an issue of the New York Times, much less purchased one. It was a newspaper that I always thought was for successful and knowledgeable people, neither of which I thought of myself as being. With it being a "holiday" issue, I knew many retailers would not be open on Thanksgiving Day. I anxiously held on to the fact that maybe, just maybe, that the gracious lady that I talked to on the phone at Barnes & Noble might have been right when she told me that issue may arrive in the afternoon before the holiday.

As I arrived there, I restrained myself from running to the back of the store where the newspapers were. My heart was racing, as if I was running a marathon. I laughed at myself as I realized what I was doing.

My feelings of excitement quickly faded. The current edition of the New York Times was there, but there was no Thanksgiving Day edition.

I asked the very professional, librarian-looking lady at the counter and she informed me she was not sure that they would receive that issue because of it being on a day that their store was not open. All hope deflated from me and I thanked her for her help.

As I left the store, my speed was more indicative of my feeling of defeat. I concluded I was going to purchase an online subscription so that we could at least read the article. I wondered whether we would see it in all its glory? After all, we did not know what the article would hold. We were not even sure how big it would be. I wondered if it would be in a tiny section that most eyes that perused the sprawling newspaper would miss. After all, there had to be major events happening in the world that were more important. Once we saw the article online, then we could decide if it was worth it to contact the archive department and request copies of the paper.

So, by now, you are probably wondering why in the world I was so reverently searching for this issue of the New York Times? Believe me when I say that I never imagined the journey that would lead me to this point! Sometimes in our lives, we cannot imagine what is ahead of us.

I can tell you where it all started because I remember the moment.

It was an average, ordinary day in November. Tim and I were both home enjoying the day when I heard Tim's phone ring. This was certainly not a surprising occurrence, but what he did next was not all that common.

I heard him dismiss the call as quickly as it had come in.

"Yeah Sure," I heard him say as a laugh slipped out of his mouth.

Before I could even ask him who it was, his phone rang again.

This time he did not hang up so quickly, but I could tell that the caller did not fully have his attention. His facial expressions were full of disbelief.

As he rolled his eyes in a disbelieving manner, he became more accepting of the phone call and agreed to whatever was mentioned.

When he got off the phone, he laughed and said, "Whatever?"

"Who was that?" I asked.

He said, in complete disbelief, "A reporter from the New York Times wants to interview me for their Thanksgiving Day issue."

I could not believe what he was telling me.

We decided we would wait and see if that was going to happen. She told him she will get in touch with him soon for a phone interview. We both laughed and shook our heads. We would believe it when we see it!

I am sure we would have forgotten all about that call and put it off as a funny hoax someone had played on us. However, that call came, and an interview was done. The reporter ended the interview saying that a photographer would be in touch to set up a time to get some photos for the article.

"Do you realize how crazy this is?" I said when he told me the date the photographer would arrive.

He smiled and said, "Yes, I do."

Early in our journey, we realized that when led in a direction that you never imagined; you smile and go with the flow! We both laughed and began moving closer to the realization and acceptance of this part of the journey.

The photographer arrived at our house on a sunny Sunday morning in November. We had concluded that this may happen. The phone interview was complete and now the pictures were to be taken.

The photographer was not a turkey hunter. He found everything he photographed very intriguing. I am sure that the life of a photographer for the New York Times is interesting. He told us of many adventures he had been on. He possessed a talent for knowing the perfect questions to ask and how to photograph what was required for the article. His enthusiasm was contagious, as he heard Tim's story and saw some of his projects that were in the works.

As his photography equipment filled Tim's man cave, I couldn't help but laugh and take some pictures of my own. From my view, seeing the room filled with mounted turkeys, deer mounts and two men talking about one man's passion, it was surreal.

We awoke very early on Thanksgiving morning. The sun had not even risen through the trees. My practice on the New York Times subscription app the night before had come in handy. I could access the article. As I looked through the content, the article, "Beguiled by a Bird," caught my eye. This had to be the article. When I clicked on the article on the iPad, the screen filled with an outstanding picture of Tim in his man cave, smiling as he does when he talks turkey.

As we sat there in disbelief, my thoughts shifted to the average, non-turkey hunting New York Times reader enjoying his morning coffee in his fancy home in a big city. I imagined his thoughts as he saw the picture of a man in camouflage surrounded by mounted turkeys and deer skulls. If he did not have a background in hunting, I wondered if he thought it was strange. I also considered the possibility that the readers were accepting of the diversified content in the paper.

Offering an authentic depiction, the article showcased Tim's deep passion for the wild turkey, emphasizing his dedication to his craft. For him, the wild turkey holds a constant presence in his life.

Little did we know that in the life that we are living in 2024, it is even more true. So much has happened in the four years this article. As I look back to that time in our lives,

I realize that was the beginning of when our journey became an unexpected roller coaster ride of sorts. A roller coaster I am happy to ride and am grateful for.

We still, to this day, laugh about the day that someone from the New York Times called to do an interview and Tim hung up on them. Luckily, their sense of humor, or lack thereof, made them redial the number and call him back one more time.

This, once again, proves that on our journey in life, we never know what surprises might await us.

Chapter 14
The Mother's Day Gobbler

In the outdoors, our mind is free. When we lose the confinement of walls, we become one with vast openness. Our mind clears and we can tune in to the elements of nature. As I sit here and write in this very moment, Tim is out with a good friend, The Judge. As they chase after a wary old gobbler, I can imagine the great time they are having and the stories they will tell when they return. The turkey woods have a way of bringing people closer together. Forever, the memories of a hunt will be told to all who will listen.

As I watch the white clouds glide across the sky, my mind meanders back to my first successful turkey hunt.

We arranged for me to go on a turkey hunt. I wanted to experience it at least once so that I could understand more about this great experience to which Tim was so passionate. He took me out to his shop to make me a pot call and striker. I looked through all the wood options he had. I picked a gorgeous piece of Flaming Box Elder because I loved its character. It was light brown with gorgeous swirls of pink, red and gray faintly coloring it. When I saw it, it reminded me of my flower garden and the stunning contrast between the mulched ground and the blooming beautiful flowers.

As he began the process, he explained each step to me. Having never paid attention before, I looked around his shop. This was where he spent countless hours working. Sometimes he would be out here early of a morning before work and he would head right back out once he arrived home. He would especially do this when he had a special project going on or if he was working hard trying to figure something out. There were small stacks of wood cut into blanks, nestled in their safe spots. Each one awaiting Tim to reveal their ability to "talk turkey". The saw dust told the story of the blood, sweat and tears shed here. The worn blades of the saws and the scuffed pieces of sand paper explained the hours of research and development. There were many tools that I had never seen before. As I looked around, each one had its own spot. I am sure that some of them, marked with specific measurements, were an important part of the call making process. These dusty benches were where the creation of his turkey calls took place. Hunters would then use them on a hunt, and they would become a cherished part of their memories. The creations from this shop became the very foundation of those hunts. To me, that is an amazing thought.

I watched the entire process and could see just how he created these beautiful calls. During my time in his shop, I learned it contains many secret treasures. These secrets are the product of many lessons learned. Here, he recreates the sound of the wild turkey. Without this sound, turkey hunting would have a whole different meaning.

Once the call was complete, Tim personalized it further. It would not be an ordinary slate pot call. On it, he painted a hen and two poults crossing a stream. This had a very sentimental meaning to me, as it depicted me and our two girls. A wide grin spread across my face as I savored the joy of a call made just for me. I was even happier that I could spend time with Tim in his shop and see just what he did with all of his time spent there.

May 7, 2004

Tim and I quietly entered the woods on this particular Mother's Day. I felt as though I was entering another world. This world differed from the world I was familiar with. Despite my previous experiences in the woods, this time felt different. Our reason for being there was unfamiliar.

After supporting Tim and his passion for turkey hunting and call making, it was time for me to see what it was all about. I would experience it firsthand. I was eager to see what the day's journey would bring.

The early morning darkness in the woods was an unfamiliar experience for me. It was quiet and the coolness of the air added to my unfamiliarity. As we moved through the darkness, each step was a challenge. My mind focused, and I hoped I would be quiet. This was important. I needed to work on my ability to glide through the woods like Tim. I tried to step where he did, as I followed closely behind. He periodically stopped to listen. He continued on, as if he knew where we needed to be. I knew he had been in those woods many times and I trusted his direction. This was reassuring, as once we entered the woods, as I had lost my sense of direction. The darkness had quickly taken that away from me.

As the sun rose, the woods came alive. It was as if every creature was awakening from a night of sleep.

Suddenly, the sound of a thunderous gobble filled our ears. This was the exact sound we had been waiting to hear. My heart pounded. A fight broke out in my head. The sound of the gobble and the pounding of my heart were competing in a great battle to gain my attention.

As light filled the woods, I became familiar with my surroundings. My eyes and ears focused as I surveyed the area ahead. I didn't realize how important these two senses would become during this hunt. They are our key attributes in this game. The only problem is that our opponent has an even better sense of sight and hearing.

We had set up in several locations, each time finding that we needed to be closer. I followed Tim's lead, hoping I could learn some valuable lessons along the way.

As we approached what would be our final set-up location, he said, "Sit down in front of that tree." It was an enormous oak tree.

He whispered, "Get ready!"

As we had practiced many times, I positioned myself with my knees up and my back against the tree. I rested my Mossberg 20-gauge pump on my knee and made sure the area in front of me was clear. I was very familiar with the gun and the scope, as Tim had me practice many times to prepare for this hunt. Gun safety is very important to him and he taught me all he knows about it. This had taken away some of the fear I once had about guns.

I focused on the view in front of me. This is where I thought the gobbler would emerge from the brush. Tim was right behind me, whispering in my ear. His voice was calming until another thunderous gobble took that calmness away.

Each time that bird would gobble, it would throw me into another heart pounding frenzy.

As the gobbles became louder, my eyes searched harder. I just wanted to catch sight of him to ensure I was in the correct position and had my gun barrel pointed in the right direction.

In an instant, his vibrant head emerged from the thick bottomland brush in front of us. Soon after I saw his head, his entire body came into view. He was in full strut.

From the viewpoint I had, he looked so big. I could never have imagined or been prepared for the feelings I would feel next. Excitement filled my body, soon followed by nervousness. Was I going to muster up any sort of calmness to shoot this gobbler? It felt like my entire body was shaking. With all the practicing and talks Tim and I had about this very moment, why did it feel so different from what I had imagined?

I had him in my sights. As he came closer, a voice broke my frenzied thoughts. It was Tim. I had become so engrossed in the struggle I had forgotten he was behind me.

Calmly, he said, "He's within range. You can shoot when you are ready."

He continued on, "Relax and squeeze the trigger when you have him in your sights."

I was waiting for the perfect shot, like I had seen on the targets Tim drew me when I was practicing my shot.

At that very moment, I locked up. It felt as if time stood still. I questioned myself. I thought I was prepared for this moment. Why had I not been able to think through the process of squeezing the trigger with the turkey in my sights?

Obviously, that was not something that I could practice until this very moment. Why had I not thought about killing the turkey?

Confusion and doubt filled my already reeling mind. It was my time, the time I had waited and prepared for. I wasn't ready. My heart sunk and sadness filled my mind. I could not help but think of how excited Tim was for me and how upset he would be if I could not squeeze that trigger. I had told him I was ready and now what was happening?

In an instant, I had to decide. What was I going to do?

As the turkey came closer, a voice once again interrupted my thoughts.

Tim said, "Shoot him!"

I knew he wondered if I was going to shoot. I, myself, was not even sure about that.

My doubts faded as my mind became one with the trigger on that gun. It was unlike any of my experiences with practice shots. I felt nothing. The sound of the gun going off quickly escaped my memory. I had no anticipation of the kick. All that faded as I squeezed the trigger. My emotions were on a roller coaster. I put the gun on safety and laid it down on the ground. Tim ran toward the gobbler. I had made an excellent shot.

As he proudly walked back to me with my bird, the look on his face was one that I had never seen before. He was so excited.

He had tears in his eyes as he mustered up the words, "You got him!"

I am sure he was wondering why in the world I was still on my hands and knees. The excitement had taken over my body. I must have been a funny sight to see.

Finally, I calmed myself down enough to get up onto my feet.

We shared a very special moment, one like we had never shared before. We were both so excited about how it had worked out.

He said, "I didn't think you were going to shoot. I didn't understand why you were waiting so long!"

At that point, I didn't have the heart to tell him what happened, as I was not even sure myself.

I replied, "I was waiting to see him like I did on that target when I was practicing. I wanted to make sure I got a good shot!"

We both laughed as we sat there and relived the hunt.

As I calmed down further from all the excitement, I replayed the memory in my mind. I knew I would need to process those feelings I had, especially if I was going to continue to hunt.

As I processed them, I came to terms with them. I realized I was a respectful hunter, having the highest level of respect for the wild turkey. I was not just hunting to kill a turkey. I was hunting to provide nourishment for my family. We did this to know where our food came from and we did it respectfully. It all made sense to me. Following through with the entire process allowed me to gain an understanding of the concept of hunting.

With my first experience, I gained a very good understanding of Tim's journey in turkey hunting. Finally, I could see it through different eyes, the eyes of a hunter. I gained a new understanding of why his passion burns so deeply. I now relate to the stories he tells me of his hunts. We now share a common understanding of the great wild turkey. I feel as though with that hunt experience; I completed a puzzle and all the pieces fell into place. The memories of my first successful turkey hunt are forever engrained in our minds. These memories we will share many times in the future.

At that very moment, I had an epiphany. I gained a new understanding of "The Chase."

MY FIRST TURKEY 2004

Chapter 15

Lesson Learned

It was a beautiful Monday in early May. I was off work and outside tending to my garden. On my days off, I enjoy spending time outdoors enjoying the beautiful weather. Gardening is a relaxing hobby I enjoy.

Tim was at work, and I was waiting for him to get home.

The sudden gobble of a turkey disrupted the tranquility of the sun and breeze. As he sounded off a second time, my heart raced. I tried calling Tim, but he was not at his desk. The thought quickly entered my mind to get my camo on, as turkey season still had over a week left and I had not gotten a bird yet. I had never turkey hunted by myself. Tim has always been with me and he always called for me as well. I had confidence I could give calling a fair shot after observing Tim's turkey calling sounds.

Running inside to prepare, I put on my hunting clothes, grabbed my gun, shells, and the special Box Elder Slate pot call Tim had made for me. With my certainty of where those gobbles were coming from, I went into the woods to see if I could outwit that old gobbler.

As I headed out the door, I tried to call Tim again and still no answer. I put my phone on silent and headed to the edge of the woods. This expedition was to be made by me, alone. My heart was racing even faster. I just stood there at the edge of the woods and listened. I wanted to pinpoint again just where he was.

Another gobble echoed through the trees! That gobble confirmed I could safely enter the woods. I quietly walked along, waiting for another gobble. There was silence. I found a tree and got set up. He had been quiet for a bit, so I tried my hand at that slate call. I made a couple of soft yelps.

My calling struck him, and he gobbled again. That gobble scared the daylights out of me. I was not expecting him to respond to my less than adequate calling skills. I thought I had scared him off. My mind was racing with thoughts. What do I do now?

I tried to think about what Tim would do when we were out hunting together.

I made my mind up to do a couple more soft yelps and see if it would strike him up again.

It did, and he had cut the distance in half. I put that call down. I knew better than to call when he was coming in that quick! My memory reminded me of several stories I had heard from turkey hunters where they said to be careful not to call too much.

I got my gun ready and faced it toward the way I thought he would appear. He let out another gobble, and he topped the hill.

When I saw him, another rush of emotions filled my body. I figured in my head at what point he was in range.

My heart almost stopped when he veered to my right. My gun barrel was no longer facing the correct way. Once his head was behind a tree, I shifted my barrel. Once he cleared that tree, I knew he was in range.

BOOM! He took off running and putting, like he had gotten scared. My mind was racing. What in the world happened? Did I miss? Thoughts of what happened were racing through my mind as I was sitting there, shocked and upset, struggling to gather my thoughts. My heart shattered into a thousand pieces. What had I done wrong?

I collected up my call, striker and gun and headed out of the woods. As I walked along, I heard him gobble again. It was coming from the direction he had run. At that point, I felt defeated.

Even with feeling defeat, a wave of relief washed over me as I realized he was unharmed and I hadn't frightened him too much.

The thought didn't even cross my mind to go back out after him. All I could think about was what if I made a bad shot and wounded him if I tried again? I felt my confidence deflate even further. I felt like I had just been on a roller coaster.

When Tim arrived home, I told him my story. As I explained everything, he looked at me in disbelief. I knew he felt my agony when I told him I had missed. He could not believe it.

He said, "Let me see your gun."

I went and got it and handed it to him. He immediately ejected the shell.

He said, "Well, there is your problem right there. These are the shells that you practice with. This is not the turkey load that we take when we go hunting."

I was heartbroken. I had grabbed the wrong shells. My mind kept going to the thought that if I would have grabbed the right shells, I probably would have gotten my first turkey by myself.

As time has passed, as I think about that story, it was an outstanding hunt and I learned valuable lessons. My sadness about the outcome has dissipated. Over time, I have realized that I came out of that expedition with some extra confidence in my turkey calling skills, my shell selection, and I have a great story to tell.

Another Lesson Learned!

Chapter 16
Are You Sure?

W hen you enter the playing field of the wild turkey, you never know what is going to happen. I have heard many turkey hunting stories from hunters where things just did not go as they planned. I suppose we all have those stories if we have been hunting turkey long enough. This is one of our stories that I think you will enjoy and may even relate to one of your own stories.

It was a beautiful spring day. As we arrived at the farm, the excitement built. We felt blessed to have another hunt together.

During pre-season scouting, Tim had learned that the turkeys were spending more time in the field in a particular area. He had decided that we would hunt the birds in the ditch where the fence row ran. This is a meandering ditch that runs throughout the farm and separates the woods from the pasture. In the scenario he had hoped for, the birds would come across the field at the fence line, like they had done many times before. We set up near the ditch. The fence and the pasture were in front of us and the woods to our backs. Tim placed a decoy out and we settled in for an exciting hunt. He felt very confident about our setup and I concurred.

The farm looked gorgeous this morning. The sky was blue, and the sun was casting light across the pasture. There was a cool nip in the air, which was very refreshing. As the sun rose through the trees to our east, the field illuminated with a warm glow. The dew-tipped blades of grass appeared to sparkle as the sun made its way to them. The world was waking up, and we felt as if we were right in the middle of it.

As Tim let out a soft tree yelp, a wary old gobbler responded with a gobble that echoed across the field.

Tim confidently said, "I think once they fly down, they will slowly make their way down the field toward us."

The gobbling continued, and it was making me extremely excited. My heart was pounding. Tim cautiously got up and stood next to one of the fence posts, watching with binoculars out across the pasture toward the gobbles. He was trying to get a glimpse of a turkey flying down.

Suddenly, he came back to me and sat down behind me. "They are flying down into the field," he said. He was hoping to lure the gobbler in our direction.

As the morning continued, there was some uncomfortable silence. I always become nervous when we cannot hear the gobbles. It always makes me feel like they are checking us out or they will sneak up on us. The more silence we heard, the more we expected to either see a white head pop up in the field or get our hearts shook by a gobble or drum of a very close turkey. Neither of those things happened for what seemed like forever.

Suddenly, out of the silence, we heard a gobble. This was just not any gobble. This gobble came from up on top of the property. It was one of those gobbles that I have learned means we are going to be moving on fast, really soon. Tim is a runner and gunner. When I say run, I mean run and run fast at that.

If I am truly honest, I am the exact opposite of a runner and gunner. The feelings of excitement and the adrenaline rush that I get when I hear a turkey, especially a close turkey, is about all my body can handle. I do not have wonderful luck with running in an excited state. I learned this the very hard way, and I knew Tim was perfectly in tune with that as well.

As Tim's face lit up with a great idea, he said, "He has gone up to the top of the flat."

He then immediately said, "I think we need to go up there."

My mind and body disagreed. I said, "Don't you think we should sit here for a bit and see if he comes back down?"

I could see his mind working, and I knew he would not agree with me.

He quickly answered, "No, get your things. Let's go!"

I questioned him one last time. "Are you sure?"

He quickly answered, "Yes".

Now, the next part of this story will be familiar to you. Remember the agonizing hunt when you first began reading this book, well this is it.

Despite my better judgement, I gathered my things and followed him unenthusiastically. You see, this is not your ordinary hill. It is a leg burning, breath stealing mountainside. As we ascended, I became increasingly irritated. I was hoping my body would get me where I needed to go.

As I trudged along, I kept telling myself I could do it.

As the distance between Tim and me became further, I became increasingly more irritated. I thought, is he going to wait for me?

After all, I had put forth the great idea of just sitting there and waiting and now look at what I was doing. I didn't sign up for mountain climbing on this hunt. I also did not sign up for the brutal bramble bush torture I was enduring.

As thoughts raced around in my head, I noticed Tim had stopped and was looking down at me.

He said, "Are you okay?"

As I stopped and looked up at him, I said, "Are you okay?" in quite a disgusted voice.

At that point, he knew I had become frustrated with his decision.

As he continued, he said, "We are almost there." He always likes to add a bit of positive encouragement to every situation!

As we arrived at the top, I stopped to catch my breath and calm down a bit. I needed a second to recover from the trip I had just put my body through.

The events that followed were nothing short of hilarious.

Tim found a location to set up. Once everything was situated, he called lightly to locate where the gobbler was. At first, there was silence. The silence that will certainly scare any turkey hunter. He waited a bit and called a little louder. I had convinced myself that the gobbler had either heard us or seen us as we climbed to the top.

Suddenly, a gobble echoed through the silence of the woods, cutting short my thoughts. This was not just any gobble, it was a gobble that sounded as if it came right from where we had just left. I realized that my wonderful advice to stay where we were might have just changed the course of this hunt. I believe the same thought crossed Tim's mind as well. It appeared as though that bird had just taken a brief detour before he came down to the sound of those hens. The only problem was that those "hens" had climbed the mountainside.

The look on Tim's face was classic. He had a look of disbelief spread across it. "Wait here. I'm going to go to see if I can see where he is." Tim went back down to glass the field.

After what seemed like forever, I could see him returning. His head hung down, and he appeared to have made a big mistake.

As he got back to me, he said, "You will not believe this."

I said, "What?" as I pretended I didn't know what he was going to say.

He said, "You were right, we should have waited him out. He is down there in the field, standing right in front of where we were sitting."

At that very moment, I gained a bit of respect for my knowledge of turkey hunting. Some would call it luck, and maybe my gut feeling was just a lucky feeling. We will never know. One thing I know is that since this hunt, Tim has asked me frequently, "What do you think?"

During this hunt, Tim ate a big old piece of humble pie! His aggressive hunting style had not served him well. Even though we did not have a successful turkey hunt, we learned valuable lessons.

As turkey hunters, we all have stories like this one. The more time you spend in the field with the turkeys, the more you learn from them. Even with the unsuccessful hunts, you still have a good story to tell. Many times, those hunts contain the greatest of lessons learned. These lessons are additional tools to add to the arsenal of knowledge that a turkey hunter must have to become successful.

Chapter 17
Double Trouble

Tim had scouted the farm and knew there were a few gobblers using the field regularly. On the morning of the hunt, under the cover of darkness, we quietly made our way up to the gate. I hoped we would not attract the attention of the cows in the field. It is always a fear of mine, especially when hunting this farm.

Tim put up a partial hunting blind in front of us to provide cover. He always made sure I was comfortable with where he'd have me sit. His patience with me has always been amazing. Even I sometimes question how he does it, as I am not the most patient person.

As the darkness faded, we heard gobbles coming from the corner of the field where the wood line and the fence met. It was just as Tim had explained to me. There were several gobbles echoing out across the field. With our set up, I was already working hard to be still. My biggest challenge in turkey hunting is remaining still, which is crucial.

Slowly, three gobblers made their way across the field. Tim was ever so slightly calling at them, trying to convince them they needed to join the "hens" at the top of the hill. They headed right in our direction.

Once they arrived at the top of the knob, they were within our view, but still too far away to shoot. Tim had brought his gun with him in case the opportunity for a double arose. That was definitely a possibility. I became extremely nervous, which is my normal reaction. I have not gotten over that initial frenzy and I am not sure that I ever will. Seeing three gobblers was more than I could handle. My heart was pounding even more than usual.

As they continued on a course right toward us, excitement built up in both of us and our nerves were on high.

I sensed some nervousness in Tim's voice as he said, "They are in range. On the count of three, shoot the bird on the left."

Fear ran through my body. I had never shot a turkey any time, except on my own terms. The questions of whether I could do this ran through my mind. I paused those thoughts when I realized how awesome it would be for Tim and me to get a double.

I prepared myself and got the bird in my sights.

Tim counted, "One, Two, Three!"–BOOM!

I immediately put my gun down, as I always do. I saw one turkey flopping.

Before I even realized what had happened, Tim jumped up and ran after the other turkey.

The moments that followed have to be, frankly, the funniest moments I have ever seen while turkey hunting.

Tim was chasing a turkey through the field.

As I first watched in shock, Tim was running with his gun in one hand and his turkey vest seat violently flailing behind him. The pursuit continued all the way from where we shot the birds at the top of the field and continued toward the south end of the field down to the ditch that separated the field from the woods.

My shock turned to laughter as I realized what a comical chase I was witnessing. It felt like a childhood cartoon replaying in my mind.

I saw Tim dive and both of them disappeared into the tall grass. I waited for what felt like forever.

Then, arising from the grass near the ditch, I saw Tim with one arm waving and the other one holding a gobbler. The excitement was unbelievable.

When he made it back up to me, we had a grand celebration of the feat we had just accomplished.

"We did it," we shouted!

The Good Lord had blessed us. Tim and I had gotten our first ever double, and to do it together was amazing! This hunt will forever remain a cherished memory for us. We'll forever tell this story.

Even now, despite his denial, I still wonder if it was my gobbler that ran away. He stuck with the story that it was his shot. Either way, it was an amazing hunt and we have wonderful memories to share.

To date, Tim and I have had the blessing of sharing two doubles together. That is as good as it gets!

Shooting turkeys and making memories!

Chapter 18
The Loss Became a Gain

It was a beautiful morning in April 2020. There was a warmth in the air as the breeze carried it across the Ohio river. The warmth was a promise of spring's arrival.

The COVID pandemic was just beginning, and the world was changing before our eyes.

In the blink of an eye, my company moved my job from office work to remote working from home. There were big changes as our team shuffled through the reality of it all. They changed protocols to implement this new scenario. Honestly, for me, it was a much needed and refreshing change to the monotony that can occur.

This particular Good Friday morning was going amazingly well. Tim and I were both off work and we had a relaxing day planned.

We loaded up the Jeep and headed back to the river for a day of adventure collecting driftwood. We loved to search through the pale-colored wood in search of the gems hidden by the test of time and changed by the harsh effects of the river water. It was like a treasure hunt. The simple nick of the wood with a saw could change the destination of any piece of wood. As we searched through, Tim used his artistic eye to decide the fate of the piece in question. Hunting for each piece was a thrill and something we enjoyed.

This morning, the sunrise was beautiful. The sun on our faces warmed us after a long, cold winter. With all the craziness in the world, it was a welcoming experience. We were relaxed and at peace, enjoying our day.

The phone call came in like a meteorite making its way to earth. It hit with just as much destruction, or at least it felt that way.

I could tell by his voice and his answers that it was not a pleasant phone call. I knew it was bad news before I was even told.

When he got off the phone, he said, "They are laying me off from my position until further notice."

I sat down in disbelief.

As the tears flowed, all I could say was, "What are we going to do?" I didn't know what else to say.

At that moment, the warmth of the sun left me, and everything became dark. My entire body felt paralyzed. It felt as though someone had hurled me into space. In the darkness, I could find nothing to grasp. The darkness made me feel forever lost, consumed by fear.

As my mind tried to process what had just happened, I tried to solve all the issues that rushed into my head. My mind was in disarray.

At that moment, our familiar way of life underwent a change. Rationality eluded me.

Being the logical thinker that Tim is, he said, "It is going to be okay."

He said, "We will come up with a plan, and we will rise above this."

It was hard for me to even imagine rising from this. That is just not how my mind functions. I did not understand what he was saying.

With his artistic mind, he could see it clearly. He had felt no option but to rise and conquer this adversity. His thought was that we would take this bad and make it good, make lemonade out of lemons. He looked at the whole situation as a path that God had created for us. A way for him to work at his artistic talents and do something that he never would have done on his own, as stepping out of his comfort zone would have been far too hard to do.

I felt terrible that he had to console me, when it was me that should console him. We sat and worked through the turbulence of emotions that we felt that day. We discussed our plans. The plans for our new way of life, the next chapter in our journey.

We were on a path that God laid out for us, and we were going to follow it. God works in mysterious ways and for that, we are grateful. When God takes your hand, you do not question it.

Life as we knew it had changed. My mind had a way of taking the worst situation and making it even more dreadful. It was a characteristic of mine, one that I was not proud to admit to. It was a trait that I knew I needed to work on. Yet, it seemed like such a hard change for me to make. Life has a way of showing us at our worst and making us contemplate how we even became this way. I couldn't help but wonder if I'm the only one who thinks and acts this way.

We can ponder all we want about what could happen. I am not proud to admit that I would do that often, more than I should. We think we can keep control of our life and keep things where we think they need to be. When life as we know it changes, it can sometimes knock us off our feet.

My mind, oh my mind, I often feel it is a cage. It takes advantage of me. It boxes me in and does not allow me to see anything but the confinement I feel. No matter how hard I try, it keeps me confined to feelings of doom. A feeling lived in my mind of which I knew I needed to overcome.

My only option was to trust. Listening to what he said, I believed. I believed we would rise from this. I followed the path.

God had laid out a plan for us. He had been planning this out for years, getting us ready for this very moment. It was not until later that we realized just how detailed it was. We were unaware of the plan during its orchestration the years prior. There was no doubt and no questions. We just followed. When one comes to realize such an amazing work, it is overwhelming.

Tim's words calmed me when I never thought being calmed was an option. It was all part of the plan.

That day, I believe we both gained just enough insight to know that everything was going to be okay. It was a feeling we felt within our very being. When you understand and see the path, everything becomes crystal clear.

I would be lying if I said that Tim and I had not talked about this in the past. Those thoughts were different. They were on our terms and allowed us to think about that option. Our minds would not allow us to even consider him leaving the comfort of a 25+ year salary job.

Sometimes we would dream about him being able to work full time on his art and his passion. We would imagine how his level of creativity could expand. But as with many "dreams", we did not allow our thoughts to go any further than that.

Little did we know those thoughts would become reality. The opportunity would present itself in a way that we would have never imagined. A presentation to which we could not deny.

Since that life-changing day, when the world as we knew it changed, we have moved in a forward motion. Tim has transformed his life into a passionate daily quest to create his art. He takes each project and immerses himself in it. Like a caterpillar when it has finished growing and begins its radical transformation into a gorgeous butterfly, he takes a piece of wood and transforms it into a beautiful work of art. As the project evolves, he focuses on its creation. He researches and lays out the project. The passion he possesses is unlike anything I have ever witnessed.

The hours, days, months and years following the call were unlike any we had known.

In the beginning, it felt as though we were starting over. As if a long-played game had ended and it was time to start anew. Things felt different, as they were on many levels. So many things to consider, as our minds were overturned.

In my heart, I knew things would be fine, but I knew I had a battle to fight. A change like this had rocked my world.

Tim is more of a move forward kind of soul. His mind gave him no option but to move forward and succeed.

It is funny how each of us is so different. While he appeared to be very positive and motivated to move forward and succeed, he was battling his own demons in his mind. The biggest question that plagued his mind was why did this happen?

Observing his evolution has taught me more than I could have imagined. The world extends beyond mere sight. Hidden things await discovery. How we navigate life holds immense significance. I didn't see this until I viewed it through the eyes of an artist. Our journey has revealed to me a better way to live, one that starts outside of the box that most of us naturally follow.

As time heals everything, this situation was no exception. As our minds could not find a reason for this, we proceeded on in a forward motion. There was no question as to what was occurring. We were being led on a journey. The greatest journey of all, one led by the hand of God.

In life, we think we have control and the power to decide our fate. In actuality, we are each on a journey. While we make certain decisions on the path we take; God, who comes in His time, not ours, controls our journey.

"He is Risen" Call

Jeremiah 29:11 (NASB)

[11] **For I know the plans that I have for you, declares the Lord;**

Plans for welfare and not for calamity to give you a future and a hope.

Chapter 19
Moments

We were very excited to have finally made our first trip to the Unicoi Call Maker's Show in 2022. We had tried many times in the past, but always had things come up that would not allow us to make the trip. It was a much-anticipated trip to meet up with old friends and a time to meet new friends who shared in the passion of turkey hunting and turkey call making.

We arrived at the quaint mountain lodge. The setting was picturesque. The mountain views were breathtaking. As the mountain tops peaked through the clouds, it was as if we were on top of the world. It was a gorgeous setting, and we were in awe of the beauty.

As we entered the lodge, camaraderie filled the air. It loomed in every corner of the building. It resembled the feelings of a family reunion, as people who had not seen each other for a long time rekindled their friendships. There were several fireplaces throughout the lodge that added to the warmth. We later learned that the fireplaces were a location of superb storytelling. The place to be if you wanted to be a part of this great gathering. The hum of excitement from all the turkey hunters was contagious. Tim was in his element, and we were enjoying the event. The best of the best were all in attendance. We had prepared feverously for the trip and Tim had a collection of calls with him to share.

The sounds of the wild turkey filled the room, as turkey calls were being put to the ultimate test. Most of the attendees had the wild turkey sound that they preferred already in their head. They were all looking for that perfect call that could bring the sound out of their head and into the air for all to hear. These were the sounds they dreamed about, the sound they each wanted to take with them in their arsenal of tools on their next turkey hunt.

In the opinion of many turkey hunters, these calls measure the success of a hunter. The hunters each have their own calls that they prefer and have learned the importance of each through trial and error during the hunting of the wild turkey. Each hunt teaches the hunter another important lesson in the game. The more a hunter hunts, the wiser he becomes. The wild turkey is one of the greatest teachers to anyone willing to listen. He will teach you everything you need to know about him. Those who have been hunting for many years have great wisdom, and the most success.

The first official day of the event was a cold and gloomy afternoon on January 14, 2022. The mountains seemed more ominous, with the fog looming over them. We couldn't clearly see their existence as we did on the sunny day that we arrived. The same excitement filled the air, and the sound of the wild turkey was even more prominent in the building. The sounds of the calls were so loud that a person could barely hear themselves talk. It was a sound that I have gained a bit of normalcy to.

However, in the beginning, it was a much different scenario. The caterwauling would get to me and I would have a sudden yearning for silence. Something I could not always attain as quickly as I liked.

The sounds of the wild turkey now no longer bother me at all. I have grown accustomed to them and they are a part of my life. I enjoy hearing them now and love to mimic them myself.

This would be a day in our journey that would become monumental to both of us. It would be a long awaited connection where two paths would cross. Tim would find the courage to do something he had wanted to do for a long time. We could have not imagined just how that decision would change our course.

With the decision to get a critique of his box call from one of the best in the business, Irving Whitt, Tim made the step toward making this happen.

Mr. Whitt had past connections with Neil Cost, "The Grandfather of Box Calls." He knew everything about box calls and certainly knew if one sounded good or not. Even being as nervous as he was, Tim knew this was something he needed to do. He respected Mr. Whitt greatly and felt intimidated to approach him.

As we stepped outside onto the large, covered porch, we noticed several rocking chairs lined up, creating a very quaint setting. The atmosphere immediately welcomed us. Even though the misty rain and cold air created an adverse feeling, we stood there and gathered ourselves.

Mr. Whitt was standing by the steps of the porch, smoking a cigarette.

As we moved closer to him, Tim had a look of second guessing on his face. I noticed it immediately and quietly made it known that he should proceed ahead. We still laugh when we think about it today.

I felt that if he had feedback from Mr. Whitt, it would be a piece of the puzzle that would allow him to go even further on his journey. You see, an artist's worst enemy lies in his own mind. I knew his call sounded good, but me telling him that was not enough. There was a definite need to receive feedback from someone who knew their stuff. I knew this would get Tim moving in the right direction and allow him to hone in further on his skills.

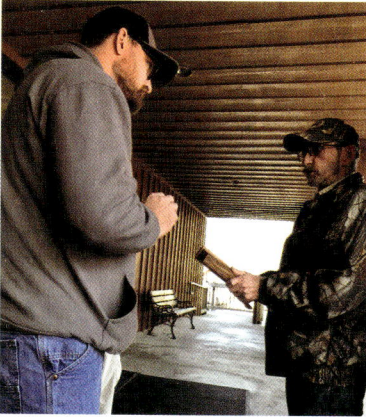

We approached him. I knew Tim would not back out now. He introduced himself and asked if Mr. Whitt would give him a critique of his call.

As Irving grabbed hold of the box call and played it, history was being made at that very moment. We did not know at the time to what degree or just where this would lead.

I could feel Tim's nervousness, as he was unsure what the outcome was going to be. He had hoped for the best and prepared for the worst.

As he played the call for what seemed like forever, the suspense was building.

As he stopped playing the call, he said, "That sounds good."

I knew at that point Tim felt a moment of relief.

He continued, "You definitely have the young hen on the left side and the old hen on the right. There is definitely turkey in it."

That moment was monumental in his career. We did not realize the friendship created at that very moment. We would find out later just how it would play out and how this single decision would further our journey.

I have always known Tim would go far. His passion is undeniably endless and his humble demeanor will take him right where he needs to be.

This meeting was the beginning of a great friendship. Irving and his wife, Darlene, are a wonderful part of our turkey call making family. They are wonderful people and we are so happy that we can call them friends.

Later in our journey, Irving was monumental in helping Tim in his process of learning to make hen boxes.

In appreciation of all of Irving's help, once Tim was happy with his first prototype of the hen box, he sent it to Irving to critique. While he was once again extremely nervous awaiting the feedback, he was happy to send it as a gift.

On the bottom of the call, Tim wrote: Prototype #1 "If bad, please return and we will pretend this never happened."

Once Irving received the call, he sent Tim a message which stated: "I am impressed with your call and it sounds great. Fixin' to give it the ultimate test next week."

Little did Tim know, his plan was to take it hunting with him.

Tim later received pictures of Irving, his turkey, and the hen box. This picture now hangs in Tim's studio as a reminder of one of the many amazing moments of our journey.

Psalm 32:8 (NASB)
[8] I will instruct you and teach you in the way which you should go;
I will counsel you with My eye upon you.

Chapter 20

Mary's Farm

As we sit looking out across the rolling hills of the emerald pasture, it appears as though the heavens reach down to touch the earth. The blue sky and soft white clouds create a mesmerizing display of nature's artistry. We feel a deep sense of awe and reverence. In moments like these, we cannot help but be reminded of the divine presence that permeates every aspect of our lives. This farm, with all its wonders, is a testament to the intricate design of God's creation.

I whisper to Tim, "This must be what heaven looks like."

He nods his head in agreement.

As the gentle breeze carries whispers of cherished memories, gratitude floods our hearts for the moments of laughter, camaraderie, and triumph that we have shared on this beautiful farm. Each blade of grass, each rustling leaf, holds within it a myriad of memories, etched in our minds and hearts, a testament to the bonds forged and indelible moments that have shaped our souls.

The following story is one of an inspirational lady and her farm.

During a hunter's life, one will search for land to gain permission to hunt. One particular farm comes to mind to me on Tim's journey to find such land. This was an amazing piece of land and an even more amazing gem living on that land.

After an initial failed attempt for permission, something made Tim try again. It was on that second attempt that Mary granted him permission to turkey hunt her farm.

Tim and I would work with Mary to help her on the farm as a tradeoff for allowing us to hunt her property. It was during this time that we learned of her great determination and work ethic. As we would bale hay and help her on the farm, we quickly learned that her intentions were to be right there working alongside us. It was amazing to see her doing the work she was doing at her age.

Mary, an extraordinary 89-year-old soul, embodies unyielding determination, boundless knowledge, and a heart that radiates kindness and compassion. In her presence, we witness resilience, unwavering work ethic, and a spirit that defies age and inspires us to live our lives to the fullest. Her dedication to the farm serves as a beacon of inspiration, reminding us that age is merely a number, and the true measure of a person lies in their determination and passion.

During our time working with Mary, close to a decade ago, she needed Tim's help to place some boards into a silo to dry. These were boards she had milled from an old cherry tree that had fallen on the farm. We did not know the impact those boards would play in our future journey.

In my mind, the convergence of all the moments experienced on the farm and the time spent with Mary have created a realization of how all things in life connect. Everything happens for a reason and at just the right moment. Our time spent here has given us a vision of God's creation. It has nourished our souls and renewed our hope. As we reflect, we see the wondrous connection.

As I sit here, I can't help but marvel at how much I have changed since my first visit to this farm. From a timid and uncertain person, I have blossomed into someone who embraces challenges and embraces personal growth. It is a testament to the power we each hold inside of ourselves. The power in us, just waiting to be found.

It has been over 10 years since that day and my life has been in a constant evolution. I have become the person who I never thought I could. Attaining courage, determination, and a true realization of this life are all traits that I now have.

In the distance, I see the daunting ridge that I once attempted to climb. Once seemingly insurmountable, it now stands before me as a symbol of my growth and resilience. The initial feelings of doubt and defeat have been replaced with unwavering determination and the knowledge that I can conquer any obstacle that comes my way. The challenges faced on this farm have taught me invaluable lessons of perseverance and the power of pushing beyond my comfort zone. Each hurdle I have overcome has not only shaped my character, but has also instilled in me the belief that I can achieve greatness.

I know that the next time I tackle that ridge, I will conquer it without a doubt.

Psalm 90:17 (NASB)

[17] Let the favor of the Lord our God be upon us;

And confirm for us the work of our hands;

Yes, the work of our hands.

Chapter 21
Chasing the Gobble

As our 4-Runner cruised down the interstate, a very familiar feeling overtook us. Our thoughts filled with excitement. Silently, both Tim and I thought of how the week ahead would progress. This feeling is one we both have felt before on our many journeys to the NWTF National Convention.

Even before Tim began competing in the Grand National Custom Callmaking Competition, we would be excited to make the journey for a weekend of "everything turkey hunting".

If we could hear our thoughts, it would be a very noisy trip. We were excited about reuniting with our turkey family. It was finally time to see everyone. It was a great convergence to Nashville. People come from all over the country for this amazing event.

This year was a very special year. It was the 50th anniversary of the NWTF. Fifty years of conservation of the great wild turkey. Tim had been thinking about this anniversary for a long time. He wanted his entry to be a salute to that very cause during this very grand event.

I remember him telling me, "It is what we all love to do, chase the gobble!"

He was absolutely right. There was no better time for this project to be born. It was perfect timing during the grand celebration of the wild turkey.

My thoughts carried me back to our trip home from the convention last year. As we embarked on our journey home, a bubbling excitement fueled animated conversations about the convention's unforgettable moments, reminiscing on the good times and, of course, we always discuss thoughts for next year's convention. We cannot get enough of it all. It is one of our favorite times of the year.

On that trip home, Tim mentioned, "Next year will be the 50th anniversary of the National Wild Turkey Federation."

He said, "I have a project that I have been thinking about for this special occasion."

He has the exceptional ability to see his pieces before he even creates them. This is an ability that I cannot fathom in my mind.

His mind, brimming with artistic inspiration, resembles an overflowing file cabinet, bursting with ideas waiting to be unleashed. Hearing about his ideas at their moment of inception as words flowing from his mouth, I cannot visualize them as he does. As he progresses in their creation, it is then that I can see them come to life. Seeing the entire process never ceases to amaze me.

Our excitement built as we arrived in Nashville. Tim felt some relief as the time drew near to deliver his project to the competition. This project that had first overtaken his mind with its inception over a year ago.

The last step is the safe delivery into the hands of the competition to be judged.

The most important part for Tim is for it to be enjoyed by all who lay their eyes on it. He loves being able to share his work with people as they journey through the show. I can honestly say that the most important part of the entire competition for Tim is to allow people to see his visions in their completed form. I suppose that is the desire of all artists.

As we entered the Gaylord Resort, familiar feelings overtook our senses. When we entered the hotel, it was like stepping into a tropical paradise. The warmth and humidity slightly caresses our face. It is a welcome feeling coming from the cold winter air outside. Every sense activates. The sound of running water draws our attention to the massive waterfall. In every direction, there are beautiful, lush green tropical plants. Hidden within these plants are gorgeous flowers peeking out to greet us. Everywhere we look, there are treasures. Orchids scale the rock walls as if they have found their perfect place here. We stop to relish in the beauty that surrounds us. We thank God for the opportunity to be here once more.

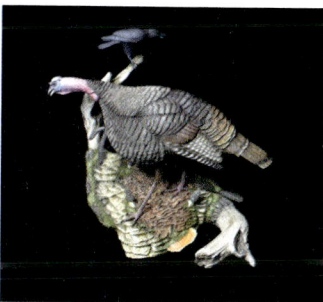

Once we deliver his piece, he has an amazing feeling of completeness. His thoughts project to the fact that he has successfully delivered yet another project for many to enjoy!

We stop and sit down to enjoy the feelings we have. As I sit here relishing in the beauty that surrounds me, I realize how encapsulated the beauty is in this building. As I look at the dome of glass above me, I realize how separate we are from the world outside. Just like Tim's pieces, each creation contains its own beauty. A part of him will forever remain with each piece.

"Chasing The Gobble" was a labor of love. A long-awaited idea in the mind of a very determined artist. Its timing was just as impeccable as its splendor. It is a representation of everything wild turkey. It is what we all long for—"Chasing the Gobble!"

Chapter 22

The Epiphany

As I sat in the front row of the ceremony, my heart was pounding. My palms were sweating, and I was slowly losing control of myself. My mind was reeling. As Tim sat beside me, I could feel his emotions. We were witnessing a pinnacle moment in his career.

In the building, I couldn't help but notice the rumble of conversation pulsating in my ears. It was a sort of relaxing sound that lulled me into a brief calmness.

My calmness disappeared when the announcer began the ceremony. This was a very important ceremony for a select group of callmakers. I was excited for them all. I was especially excited about the fact that Tim was about to be inducted into the NWTF Grand National Custom Call Competition's Hall of Fame. It was a grand accomplishment, and I knew how long and hard he had worked to get to this point.

The Merriam-Webster dictionary defines Epiphany as "a sudden striking understanding of something." Most of us will have an epiphany during our journey through life. Some of us will have more than one epiphany and, I also suppose, it is quite possible for some to never experience an epiphany. It is possible to never understand the journey we have been on or to perceive it as anything at all. While we do not know when or if this epiphany will occur, we continue our journey with a "feeling" that something great will happen. We have faith that just around the corner, good will come. This gets us through the dark and dismal times of our lives. The times when our course seems to change in an unfavorable direction. During these times, it is our perception of the situation that denotes the direction in which we go. If we change our perception of the situation, we change the situation itself.

As the announcer began short stories on each of the call makers that were being inducted, he purposely left out the names at the beginning of the description. This was an ingenious approach to the ceremony. Would I be able to recognize when he told Tim's story? I listened carefully as he began announcing. After announcing several callmakers, the announcer began another introduction:

"The following inductee has the ability to capture nature in its truest form in each of the pieces that he enters into the competition year after year. His artistic approach makes him not just an artist, but a storyteller for nature's most beautiful moments."

My heart was racing. I had chills running throughout my entire body. All I could think about was the journey we had been on and how extremely nervous Tim must be. Other than Tim himself, I was the only one who knew how hard he had really worked to get to this point. I knew of the hours and the passion he had extruded from every inch of his being. I knew how truly grateful he was to be here at this very moment and how important this piece of the puzzle was for him.

The announcer continued on, "His accomplishments are not just defined by his artistic ability, though. He is highly respected among his peers, exemplifies what good sportsmanship should be, always has a positive outlook on everything, and is willing to help any callmaker who wants to be better. He is strongly invested in this competition with his five Best of Show awards in decorative turkey, countless class trophies, and over 100 category placement medallions. I would like to welcome the one and only, Tim Oldham, Jr., up on stage to accept his place in the Hall of Fame."

As he proceeded to the stage, I imagined how he must be feeling. My tears were flowing like a river. My heart was so proud. It felt as if it was about to burst right out of my chest. My face was wet with tears and my shirt was showing the signs. I did not care. This was a monumental moment, and I would not spend it fighting off tears.

I thought of how his endless passion for the wild turkey had brought him to this very stage.

He humbly received his award and there were pictures taken. At that moment, I knew why I was in the front row. I would not have missed this moment for the world. The smile on Tim's face said it all. I knew he realized that all of his long hours spent for the competition, his blood, sweat and tears going into creating these elaborate calls and his quest to make them sound amazing were not in vain.

It was at this moment that I experienced an epiphany. This was like none I had ever experienced. The years of hard work, trials and tribulations were culminating into a glorious moment, a much-deserved moment, and I knew what it all meant. Thinking back to all the things that had happened over the last few years, I couldn't help but take a moment to realize how much he had been through, how much we had been through.

Through all the trials, his faith never wavered. His undying passion remained steadfast, and we continued on our journey in a forward motion. We never looked back on what had happened and only looked forward to the future. We knew that, despite all that had occurred, we were on a journey directed by God, with a planned path we were to follow with a strong faith in its direction.

As the photographer was taking pictures, Tim and I made eye contact and he pointed at me. I knew he was giving me the most heartfelt "thank you" that he could give. I accepted it wholeheartedly.

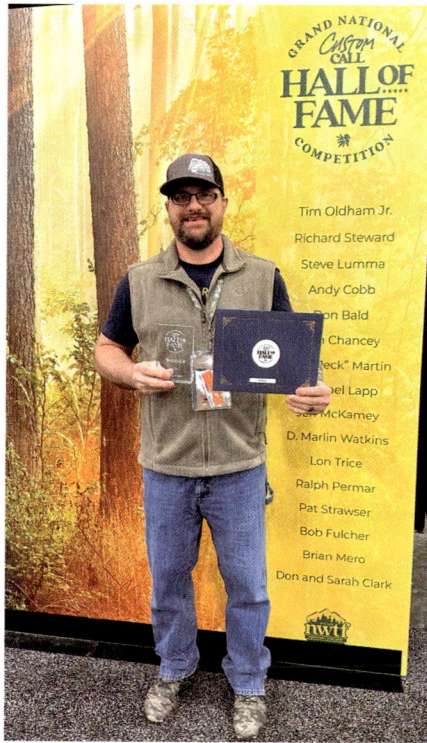

Chapter 23

I Did It!

The Epic Hunt

We jumped out of bed before the alarm sounded. It was the opening day of Indiana spring turkey season 2024 and we were excited.

Over coffee, we finalized our plans for the hunt. I felt different this morning than I have in the past. An excitement like no other filled my mind. My usual feelings of doubt about missing a turkey or messing up a hunt were nowhere to be found. In their place were feelings of enthusiasm and confidence.

In February of this year, I started collecting trumpet calls from friends of ours who are callmakers. I had been practicing for months, working to better my calling skills. This season, I had decided that I was going to call my turkey in using one of my new trumpets. If I could pull it off, it would be a first for me, as Tim has always called for me in all but one hunt, a hunt which was unsuccessful.

The decision to take on the responsibility of calling a turkey in myself was a turning point for me. It showed how my confidence had grown over time and how I will challenge myself to achieve new accomplishments.

We enjoyed using calls we have collected from our fellow friends. Using their calls during our hunts is a way to "take them with us on our hunt". It is a reminder of the connections and relationships formed through our passion for turkey hunting. The hardest part was deciding which calls I would take on the hunt with me. I chose a Val Espinoza trumpet and a Scott Basehore cane yelper.

The golden rays of the sunrise painted the landscape in hues of orange and pink, casting a warm glow over the trees. A gentle rustling of leaves and the soft whispers of the wind lulled me into a state of calm, preparing me for the hunt ahead. Smelling the fresh dew and earth permeating the air invigorated my senses as I settled into my spot in the woods.

As my ears filled with the sounds of the joyous birds singing their morning songs, it was as if nature were celebrating this moment. I sat back and soaked in all of its beauty.

After about an hour, Tim got up to see if he could see anything in the open area that was out of our vision. I watched him as he eased up to glass the field.

As he motioned for me to join him, the look on his face told me the hunt was about to begin.

As I approached him, he said, "There are two birds down the way, but they are heading away from us."

These birds did not have hens with them, which was a good sign.

He continued by saying, "We will have to go down to the low spot and cut across to the woods on the other side."

Feelings of excitement and nervousness enveloped me. It was a blend of anticipation and exhilaration that made my heart race.

With our move closer, we had cut the distance down, but the birds were still 200 yards away. Tim confirmed it was indeed a Jake and a Gobbler.

My heart raced with anticipation as my once imagined thrill of calling in a turkey using my newfound trumpet skills was a step closer to coming true. All the time I spent practicing would come down to this very moment. The realization that this hunt could mark a milestone achievement for me filled me with a sense of purpose and determination.

As I pursed my lips around the trumpet, the sound of a few soft yelps echoed through the quiet woods, beckoning the turkeys to heed its call.

Tim said, "A little louder."

I did just that and, as I did, those two birds threw their heads up and proceeded in our direction. The gobbler went into full strut. Excitement overtook my body.

Tim said, "Try again!"

I did and the thunderous gobble that reverberated through the air was a testament to the power of my calling, a moment that sent shivers of excitement down my spine.

I tried again, a little louder, enticing them further. They continued to move in our direction. I couldn't believe that they responded to my calling. With each step closer, the weight of the moment grew, as if the very essence of the hunt hung in the balance.

The tension mounted as the turkeys closed the distance, 100 yards, 50 yards, 40 yards. I couldn't believe my eyes. It was working! I was calling them in!

As I aimed at the gobbler, a strange mix of confidence and focus washed over me. It was as if all my doubts and uncertainties had vanished. I felt in control. I knew what I needed to do.

With a pounding heart, I got that gobbler in my sights.

Tim said, "He is in range. Wait until he steps away from the Jake!"

When he stepped away, I confidently squeezed the trigger!

With a resounding BOOM, the shot echoed through the woods, symbolizing the culmination of my months of practice and determination.

As that turkey fell to the ground, a surge of triumph washed over me. I had accomplished my goal.

I DID IT!

With a pounding heart, I took a moment to appreciate the significance of the shot. It represented not only the culmination of my calling skills but also a personal triumph over self-doubt and fear.

The overwhelming excitement that followed was a mix of adrenaline, joy, and satisfaction that filled my being. It was a moment of pure elation knowing that I had achieved what I set out to do.

The memories made on this hunt will forever hold a special place in my heart. The sense of accomplishment and the shared experience with Tim created a bond that transcended the act of hunting. It was a true blessing.

THIS PICTURE SAYS IT ALL!

Looking back at the journey from doubt and hesitation to confidence and success, I realize that the distance I have traveled as a hunter mirrors the distance I have traveled within myself. It is a testament to the power of perseverance and believing in yourself.

This hunt served as a reminder of the importance of pushing past limitations. It has taught me that growth and success often lie just beyond the boundaries of comfort and familiarity.

Chapter 24
Where Do We Go From Here?

S o far, this journey has been one of many emotions. There have been overwhelming challenges that tested our resilience. We have experienced moments of pure bliss and heart-wrenching sorrow. Like the seasons, these moments transition from one to the next. There have been unexpected events and hard-earned accomplishments. Some moments ended up working out for the best, even though they were tough to understand at the time they happened. There has been fear of the unknown, which was replaced with faith for the future.

As Wayne Dyer once said, *"When you change the way you look at something, what you look at changes."* On our journey, I gained a great understanding of this.

During times of trial, as the ones we were facing, we realize that the only thing we truly have control of is ourselves. We cannot control the external factors that will certainly come into our life. Each of us has the amazing ability to control ourselves, our thoughts, our perception and most of all our attitude. We must only conquer the battle in our minds and see ourselves prevailing. We must change our perception. This only requires from us, the will to accomplish our goals.

I must admit that I wasn't used to my mind functioning in such a way. It wasn't until I watched Tim carry out the process that I realized more about the strength and the power of the mindset. He had lived his entire life this way. Why was it I had never understood this? While I still do not understand why this theory was unknown to me in my 50 years, I am certainly blessed to see it now.

Through our journey, I encountered this theory of mindset in various ways. I have realized that everything lies within our reach. We must only go for it in a way that we see it manifesting in our minds. Our infinite subconscious mind only requires that we see what we want and that we have faith that we will get there.

I believe people enter our lives for a very particular purpose. It may take time for us to discover. In good time, we will see it. As the pieces of the puzzle fit together, we make an amazing discovery. It will come from places that are least expected and it will most certainly affect the trajectory of our life. Everything will come together as a well-written story.

You will learn things about yourself that you never dreamed could be true. As L. Frank Baum wrote in the story, *The Wonderful Wizard of Oz*, and as Glinda the Good Witch told Dorothy, ***"You've always had the power, my dear, you just had to learn it for yourself."*** This is a perfect example of the power we all carry inside ourselves to accomplish great things. We must only channel our own inner strength, courage, and determination.

Since I began writing this book a year ago, my understanding of our journey has presented itself to me. The plans and our path have been further explained by a sequence of events that have occurred. These events have allowed me to see clearer. I owe the ability to write this book to the power of understanding my mindset. I believe that without this understanding and the will to document our journey for future generations, I would not have taken this part of the journey.

Looking back, I can see how my conservative approach to life hindered my ability to take risks and experience new opportunities. My fear of failure has always held me back.

Through introspection, I have uncovered my true passion and aspiration. I have always had a deep love of writing. Through self-reflection, I realized my fears held me back from pursuing that passion. I am now chasing my writing dreams.

Life is an amazing journey. Just as the sun travels around the earth providing light, our journey unfolds in its own time, right before our very eyes.

I say to you, go out and achieve your goals, see them manifesting. Live life to the fullest. After all, we only have this one life to live.

So, to answer my question, "Where do we go from here?" We go wherever we wish to go. We only need to have the will and we will accomplish great things!

Chapter 25
Thank You All

As I near completion of writing this book, my heart fills with love. I have enjoyed putting our memories onto the page for anyone who wishes to read it. This time has allowed me to realize the true amazement this entire journey has given us. Even though there have been some difficulties, it truly has been a wonderful ride.

While this certainly isn't the end, I have gained a great sense of hope for the future.

From the very beginning of our great journey, we have enjoyed sharing our hunting memories and hearing the stories of others. From the shared hunts, the stories, the turkey calls and the carvings, the flame of passion burns bright. The glow it emits rivals that of a sunrise peeking through the turkey woods during an eagerly awaited hunt. A hunt eternally etched in our memory. A hunt we will share with many fellow hunters, as we relive it through the flames of a campfire. Those bright orange flames will take us back to that sunrise that warms us. A memory of the flames burning in our soul that fuels our passion. As with each story we hear or tell, there is a lesson to be learned. With these great lessons, we only become a better warrior in the turkey woods.

In reality, I could not mention every single soul who played a part in our journey. With that being said, please know that we thank every single one of you who has played any sort of role at all in our story.

From the people we have briefly met, to those we see annually at big events, and to those who have played a significant role in our journey, please know that we feel blessed to know you and we appreciate your friendship more than you will ever know. Without each of you, our story would not be a story at all. Regardless of the duration, we treasure the time we spend with you. We pray each one of you experiences many blessings on your journey through life. We hope our paths continue to cross on this great journey.

For those who are no longer with us, we consider ourselves blessed to have known you during your time here on earth. We will continue to hold the memories of you closely in our hearts. We will continue to share these memories with others.

For all of you out there that we have not yet met, those who will be a part of our future journey, we anxiously await your arrival, in great hopes our paths cross. We look forward to meeting you and sharing stories.

For those of you who we already call friends, our great friends in the "turkey family", we look forward to further nourishing our friendship and sharing even more experiences with you.

Thank you!

Chapter 26
To Our Grandsons

April 30, 2024

To Our Precious Grandsons,

To say we are excited to have each of you in our family is an understatement. We have lived for this day when we can tell you just how precious you are to us. Not to say that we wanted time to flow away from us, as the waves in the ocean, but to be present at this very moment is special for us.

We have journeyed through time picking up bits of knowledge and carrying on with our passions, building up to the point we are today. In doing this, we have an enormous amount of knowledge to share with each of you. We believe that this knowledge will open doors for you, allowing you to embrace your passions and dive deeper into your interests. We hope to show you many exciting opportunities exist in the world, to give you the chance to pick any of those that you so choose.

In saying that, we want you each to know that we will not be partial to whatever decision you decide to make. We will back your choices as if they were our own, just as we did with your mothers.

We hope you decide to take the road less traveled and the road that leads you to nature and all the joys we have found there. We hope you each find your own individual passion and dive right into it, knowing that there are no limits in what you can do. All you must do is have a will to do whatever you love. It is that, along with a great deal of faith, that will lead you on your journey. When things do not seem to go in your favor, hold tight to your faith. This will lead you to your dreams.

We love each of you to the fullest and will always be here for you, no matter the circumstances. Know we love you with all our hearts and we are so proud to be your grandparents.

We love you each more than you will ever know.

Love,

Nonni & Poppi

Kawhi & Krue 2024

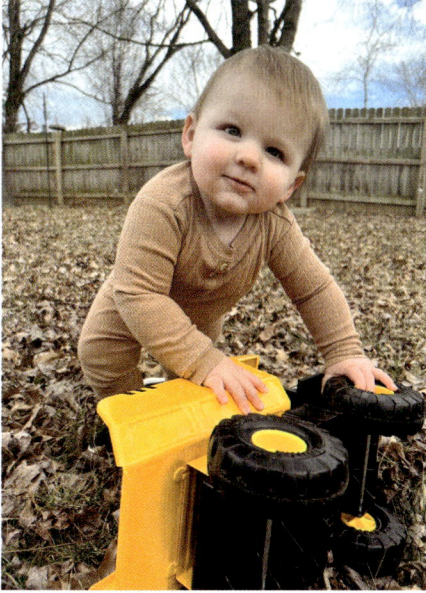

Granger 2024

Chapter 27
Through The Years

W hen I think back to these competition entries, I can't help but have a feeling of closeness with each one. I know the amount of dedication each one required is unimaginable to me.

As Tim and I have discussed, it is like each piece grows into a part of us during their creation. We watch them morph into the beautiful piece they become. We then set them free, as we do with our children. Each piece has its own life, its own meaning, and certainly its own set of trials and tribulations.

I can only imagine the feelings that Tim has for each one. As he begins a piece, he pours every bit of himself into it. He spends hours upon hours with it during its creation.

Here is a look through the years at Tim's six Earl Mickel Award winning pieces.

"Close Call" – NWTF 2016

"Roosted" – NWTF 2018

Earl Mickel Best of Show Decorative Turkey Calls

"The Boss" – NWTF 2019

"Mother's Love" – NWTF 2020

"Rattled" – NWTF 2022

"Chasing the Gobble" – NWTF 2023

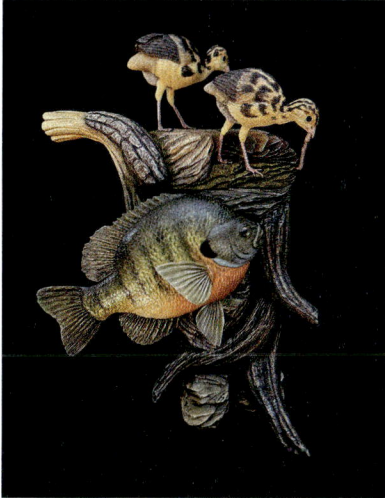

"The Early Bird Gets the Worm" – NWTF 2024

Us, through the years

NWTF CONVENTION 2014

NWTF CONVENTION 2024

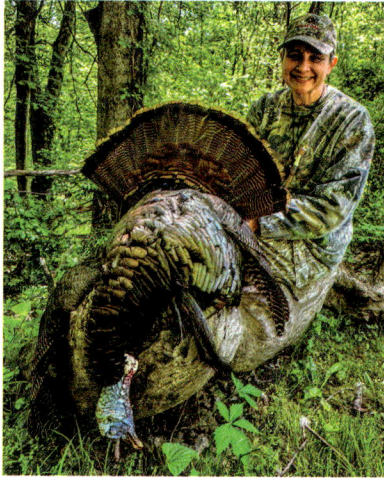

I DID IT! – APRIL 2024

TIM'S "BISCUIT BIRD" – APRIL 2024

Acknowledgements

Through my journey in writing this book, there are more people than I have room to thank. Many people have supported me during this process, and I am forever grateful.

Foremost, I thank God for leading me on this journey.

To Tim, you never doubted me. You have been with me throughout this entire journey. Thank you for the endless hours of reassurance and the reading you have done for me. When I wanted to stop and give up, you were there to lift me back up and move me forward. I am blessed to have you in my life. Your amazing God-given gifts have allowed me to have a story of an incredible journey to write about. The day I met you was the day my life changed forever. My heart overflows with gratitude for having you as my husband.

To Courtney, Corey, Kawhi, Krue, Caitlynn, Kegan and Granger, you have all made my life the greatest story to tell. I love being Nonni. It is my number one honor. Thank you for your never-ending support. You never doubted me through this journey and for that, I am forever grateful.

To Mom and Dad, thank you for giving me a great foundation. My years growing up were the most magical time, and I am forever thankful to have you both. Thank you for your constant support in all that I do.

To Brent Rogers and the Mossy Oak Bottomland Book Club seminar at the NWTF convention in 2023 and 2024. Thank you for your inspiration. It was attending that first seminar in 2023 that ignited my deep inspiration to write this book. Thank you, Brent, for your amazing contribution to the world of literature and your great endeavor to preserve the heritage of everything wild turkey. Your encouragement and insight along the way has been amazing. I appreciate you.

To Don and Sarah Clark, thank you for your friendship and insight into writing my book. It was great to have someone to talk to who had been there. I appreciate all the questions answered and the help you have given me.

To Michael T. Simpson, thank you for your amazing contributions to the writings on the great wild turkey and your endless help when I asked what seemed to be endless questions.

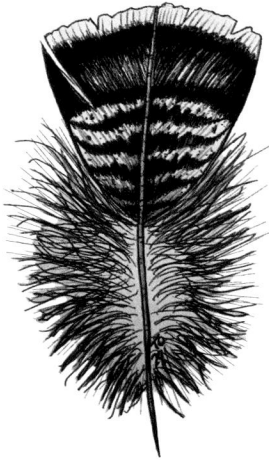

About the author

Mindy Oldham is from Newburgh, Indiana, where she has lived most of her life. Her love for the outdoors began at a very young age, when she would play outside every chance she could. She loves exploring in the woods and enjoys being out in nature. She has a passion for gardening and has since she was a young child, when she would help her grandfather with his vegetable stand.

After marrying the love of her life, Tim, she moved only a mile from the home where she grew up. She enjoys hunting with Tim. They enjoy living off the land in any way that they can. They enjoy traveling in their free time.

She became the mother of two amazing daughters. She has a great love for her family and especially her three grandsons.

This is the first book that she has written.